MW00825024

99 BOTTLES OF WINE™

THE MAKING OF THE CONTEMPORARY WINE LABEL

TEXT BY DAVID SCHUEMANN
FOREWORD BY AGUSTIN HUNEEUS SR.

VAL DE GRACE BOOKS, INC.
NAPA, CALIFORNIA

Published by Val de Grâce Books
Napa, California
www.valdegracebooks.com

CF Napa Brand Design
2787 Napa Valley Corporate Drive, Napa, CA 94558
(707) 265-1891 | www.cfnapa.com

© 2013 CF Napa Brand Design, LLC

All rights reserved. No part of this publication may be reproduced or transmitted in any form or by any means, electronic or mechanical, including photocopying, recording, or any information storage or retrieval system, without permission in writing from the copyright holders.

All wine labels reproduced in this book are the exclusive property of the respective wine companies and may not be copied, used or adopted in any way without their written permission. The appellation information listed for each wine company applies to the wines that are featured and does not necessarily encompass all of the appellations within the wine brand's portfolio.

99 Bottles of Wine™ is a registered trademark of CF Napa Brand Design, LLC

Photo Credits: All photography by Tucker & Hossler except photos found on pages 6, 18, 108, 109, 185 and 189. Photo on page 161 by Dan Mills.

ISBN 978-0-9848849-4-0
Library of Congress Control Number: 2013930526
Printed by Toppan Leefung Printing Limited, China

22 21 20 19 18 17 16 15 14 13   10 9 8 7 6 5 4 3 2 first edition

Contents

The Spirit of Wine

By Agustin Huneeus Sr.
The renowned creator of Quintessa wine

As part of human culture for thousands of years, the crafting of wine has long been considered one of the highest expressions of agricultural development and even the measure of a civilization's refinement. Wine first came to America with the first European missionaries and colonists, and with eloquent champions like Thomas Jefferson and Benjamin Franklin, wine took root in American culture and slowly grew into a mainstay of modern American life.

The United States, in turn, has had a profound impact on the much wider world of wine. It was here, for instance, that we started naming wines according to their dominant varietal, as opposed to their place of origin. It was here too that numerical systems for ranking the quality of wines were invented—a development that has greatly influenced the marketing and sales of wine worldwide. The US wine industry has also advanced the globalization of wine. Traditionally, local consumption was almost always limited to local wines. For instance, if you went to a restaurant in Bordeaux and asked for a wine from Burgundy, you might well be shown the door! The fact that today you can go to a restaurant and order a wine from almost anywhere is largely due to the reach and power of the American way of wine. As in the realms of food, fashion and music, you can also see strong US influence in the rise of the New World wines that are now being crafted in places like Australia, New Zealand, South Africa, Argentina and my native Chile.

And so it is with the art of the wine label. Historically in Europe, wines were not sold by brand or varietal. Instead, the name of the wine was most commonly derived directly from the wine property, and the labels on the bottle typically featured some aspect of the property itself, such as an etching of the estate's château or the family's coat of arms. We can pinpoint the moment when that tradition began to change. It was in 1945 when the Baron Philippe de Rothschild, the innovative owner of the Château Mouton Rothschild in Bordeaux, began using the art of celebrated artists on his labels. From that point forward, the Baron Philippe featured provocative artwork on his labels from painters like Pablo Picasso, Georges Braque, Marc Chagall, Salvador Dali, Joan Miró, Andy Warhol and many more. Picasso's contribution was in itself a shocker. It featured a stunning Cubist painting of a woman, and it marked a true breakthrough in the art of the label and in the much wider culture of wine.

Today we can see it clearly: The departures from tradition in our wine culture are dramatic—and accelerating. As you will discover in the pages ahead, today we have wines with capricious names like "Slingshot," "Boneshaker" and "Old Ghost," and they have fresh, surprising labels to match. Even the way wine is packaged is now being reinvented. We try wine in boxes, in pouches and even in handy, ready-to-pour glass carafes. Some ideas click; some ideas quickly disappear. That is the American way. In the US, we innovate. We challenge. We test tradition, and if the old ways of doing things no longer suit our purposes or our times, we happily discard them.

I have watched the evolution of wine and wine labels over a long period of time and from a personal, hands-on perspective. I started out in the wine business in Chile, where I was born. Our wine culture in Chile was modeled on the Bordeaux tradition. When I was twenty-eight years old, I was running what was then a small wine company, Concha y Toro. Back then, in the 1960s, the label was not as important as it is today because only about five percent of our wine in Chile was sold in glass bottles. The rest was sold in bulk, in different formats. Stores, for instance, would sell our wine from a huge wooden barrel with a little spigot on it, and consumers would come with their own container and fill it up.

Change came to us in unexpected ways. One day, for instance, we had a visit from a government official. It turned out that a small competitor was challenging the name we were using and, to our surprise, had obtained an order restraining the sale of our wine. So in order to stay in business, I was pressed to invent a new name right on the spot. The result was Casillero del Diablo, which translates as "The Devil's Locker." That name created an immediate uproar in Catholic Chile, and soon I had the archbishop and other dignitaries up in arms, crying: "You can't put the word 'Devil' on a wine label!" We refused to back down, though, and something incredible resulted. Our new label created a terrific stir, and soon our wines sold so well that our company became the market leader!

This taught me a crucial lesson: the name of a wine and its label are critically important to any wine's ultimate success.

Years later, when I took over Franciscan Estates in the Napa Valley in the mid-1980s, I learned another lesson about the importance of wine labels and packaging design. At the time, Franciscan had an enormous excess of inventory, coupled with an equally enormous shortage of cash. Our backs were to the wall; we had to find a way to sell our wine and immediately generate cash. So I created the brand Estancia, and for it we crafted a label that was very simple but also dramatic and elegant. It was a shiny metal plate in a Burgundy color with the name Estancia highlighted in gold. With some labels there is an immediate click, an indefinable touch of magic, and all of a sudden you just know that it will work. The Estancia label proved to be just that.

Today, with so many big corporations in the wine business, there are many executives and marketing specialists who dream of turning their wine into a dominant national brand, some new icon of US consumer life. Fortunately, though, two powerful forces work against that happening. First, the restaurateur, the sommelier, the wine writer and the corner wine shops—none of them want only a handful of brands dominating the wine market. Their livelihood depends on there being a wide assortment of wines and labels to offer, feature and recommend. Providers want to be able to offer wines at a wide spectrum of price, from a quick eight-dollar spontaneous purchase to a luxurious, connoisseur's wine that commands $150 a bottle or more. Offering such a spectrum keeps the wine industry open to a wide family of consumers, both in terms of what they have to spend and in terms of their own evolving knowledge and appreciation of wine.

But there is something else that prevents wine from being branded and sold like other consumer products: the spirit of wine. Wine, at its heart, is a deeply personal endeavor. Wine is exploration. Wine is feeling. Wine is taste, and everyone's taste and feeling for wine is somewhat different. As a result, a wine consumer is, by nature, not a consumer that you can turn into a customer who is constantly loyal to just one brand. Wine drinkers seek out a wide variety of wines, depending on their mood, the occasion, their passions, or just what they are having for dinner. That is the beauty of wine and why it is unique. Very few wine lovers are content to stick to a single brand, as they might with a beer or a whisky. Instead, they love to constantly explore, taste and try something new.

The spirit of wine has deeper dimensions as well. For winemakers like me, what is inside the bottle is far more than a beverage. For us, wine is art. Wine is culture. Wine has aesthetic dimensions that no other consumer product can claim. For us, wine is sun and soil. It is that very special flowering that emerges each year from our vision, our vineyard and from the passion, skill and hard work of the many people it takes to till our land, tend our vines, nurture our grapes, bring in the harvest and then slowly, patiently, lovingly, turn our fruit into the finest of wines.

As I have learned over the years, many different factors influence how people feel about and appreciate a wine. The location and architecture of the winery, the beauty of the vineyard, the shape of the bottle, the reviews that people have read about the wine, and the warmth of the welcome you extend to visitors in the tasting room—all these factors greatly influence the sensual experience of enjoying wine.

The same is true of the label. As every winemaker knows first-hand, the label on the bottle has enormous significance because its design—with the imagery, feeling and information it conveys—has a profound impact on the way a wine buyer and drinker respond to a particular wine. The label even influences the palate.

With so much at stake, creating a label and packaging that properly convey a winemaker's vision and spirit, or a specific wine's character and

personality, is not just an extraordinary challenge. It is also a subtle and complex exploration, and it is a daunting creative mountain that is very difficult to climb. To get a label right, I believe that the winemaker and the designer have to develop a special bond and a deep mutual understanding, one where they listen intently to each other as they move forward in common cause. Even then, it takes patience and commitment, and as with any art form, no amount of group thinking or consumer testing can ever guarantee the desired result. The spirit of wine demands something far more potent and always more elusive: that sudden, illuminating spark of inspiration that leads us to the soaring, indefinable feeling of "Wow!" that true art stirs inside us.

AGUSTIN HUNEEUS SR.

Introduction

By David Schuemann
Owner & Creative Director of CF Napa Brand Design

It is an exciting time in the wine business. The US is now the largest consumer of wine in the world, and wine is being produced in all fifty states. Wine's popularity worldwide is also at an all-time high, with new brands from every corner of the world flooding the market every single day. In the US alone, 120,000 new wine labels were approved by the Alcohol and Tobacco Tax and Trade Bureau (TTB) in 2012, making the marketing of wine and the need to stand out in the crowd more challenging and important than ever.

One of the keys to success in breaking through this ever-growing crowd of offerings is exceptional design and packaging. There is no question about it: with all sorts of consumer products, visually-appealing packaging piques our interest and invites trial. But in the worlds of wine and food, the art of design engages a fascinating additional truth:

We eat and drink with our eyes.

As any experienced chef will tell you, the presentation of food on the plate, the melody of colors in play and even the different textures of the food all have a significant impact on how we appreciate our dining experience. These factors influence the taste of food on the palate, and not surprisingly, the same is true of wine.

At CF Napa Brand Design, we have seen time and time again how a consumer's perception of a wine—its color, its bouquet and its taste—is profoundly influenced by the package's design, bottle shape and even the texture of the label. We have seen consumers detest a wine if it comes from a design they do not like, and we have seen the exact same consumers love the same wine when it comes from a bottle and label design that they find pleasing to the eye. Packaging that appeals to us beckons us to try a wine, reinforces our

experience of the wine while we consume it and enhances our ability to recall a brand for future repurchase. Thus, getting the design and packaging of a wine brand exactly right is not just an aesthetic exercise, it is also a commercial necessity.

In the following pages, I share a small selection of the many hundreds of successful wine labels and brands that CF Napa has created through the years. Like people, each wine brand is unique, with its own personality, history and story to tell. To provide the fullest possible picture, I have detailed the backgrounds of the wineries and the people behind them, before unveiling the design concepts and market positioning that were built into each of the packaging solutions. Vivid photography shows how all these elements flow artfully together to complete the story.

Though the labels and packaging solutions that we present here are wildly different from one another, there is a common thread behind each one: CF Napa's methodology in creating these successful brands. That methodology is based on one fundamental lesson we have learned: Differentiated strategic positioning and evocative design are both essential for establishing an emotional and cognitive connection between consumer and brand. When historical truth, culture, lifestyle and strategic positioning are balanced correctly in artful design, the results are both visually appealing and commercially successful.

To create a label and packaging that serve both the aesthetic and commercial ambitions of a wine or winery, we begin by uncovering a "brand's essence." By that I mean the underlying values, guiding principles, and hidden attributes that are at the core of the brand and what make it unique.

As a first step to this end, we sit down with our clients and listen carefully to their dreams and ambitions and to the story behind their enterprise and brand. We probe gently to identify the core elements that define their product and make it stand out from its competitors. We also like to visit the winery property to get a feeling for the place and its aesthetics. Once those core elements have been given focus, we incorporate our own wealth of consumer insights, cultural understandings and market expertise. Through this process, a concise brand story is brought to life and provides the foundation for us to create exceptional design solutions. Getting this foundation established is key, because even the most exceptional design and technique will never hide a poor idea.

In this day of everything digital, many readers might find our next step to be rather surprising— we start with sketches drawn by hand. This allows us to quickly explore ideas and provides a direct, tactile feel that we would not get from a computer. From those initial sketches, we slowly evolve our various design concepts for a given brand, and then we narrow down the field to polish our final concepts digitally. Next we refine, and often refine

some more, until we finally attain a design and packaging solution that catalyzes that all-important emotional and cognitive connection between brand and consumer. In other words, positioning the wine in direct correlation to the consumer's lifestyle, beliefs, interests and aspirations and taking the consumer on a journey from awareness of the product, to the first trial, to advocacy and, ultimately, to enduring brand loyalty.

I started designing wine labels in 2000, and since then the art of wine design and what constitutes a successful wine label and package–from the visual to the physical product–have evolved in many exciting ways. The pace of change is rapidly accelerating as wine grows in popularity and new wineries and wine brands appear every day. The future of wine packaging is sure to be filled with change, providing a challenge to the industry both aesthetically and emotionally. Yet at CF Napa we believe, fervently, that the core elements of what make a wine brand distinctive and successful are rooted in eternal truths about art, culture, and branding, and those truths remain steadfast and immutable.

DAVID SCHUEMANN

99 BOTTLES OF WINE™

THE MAKING OF THE CONTEMPORARY WINE LABEL

Old Ghost

COMPANY   KLINKER BRICK WINERY, LODI, CALIFORNIA
APPELLATION   LODI, CALIFORNIA

There is something magical about Old Growth Zinfandel vines.
Their trunks are thick and gnarled from years of maturing, and
their cordons or "branches" are always weathered and expressive.
Such are the ancient Zinfandel vines at the Klinker Brick Winery
in Lodi, California; they have roots tracing back to the early
1900s. Klinker Brick's owners, Steve and Lori Felten, are the fifth
generation of their family to care for these one-hundred-year-
old vines that produce the exceptional grapes for Klinker Brick's
signature wine, Old Ghost.

For the label, we drew our inspiration directly from those ancient
vines. To bring forth their magic, we envisioned them shrouded
in the low-lying fog of the early morning. As the central icon for
the brand, we chose the ghostlike image of a single, head-pruned
Zinfandel vine. To convey the mystical quality, the vine was
stamped in white foil and overprinted with subtle tones of gray.
The shadows of the vine were also embossed, inviting you to run
your fingers over the vine's ancient twists and textures, giving
you a tactile sense of the wine's age and strength of character.
This ethereal imagery is set forth on a canvas filled with airy
white space and subdued, classical typography. With these highly
refined elements, the Old Ghost label tells the story of this Old
Vine Zinfandel far more eloquently than words alone ever could.

OLD GHOST

LODI 2003

OLD VINE ZINFANDEL

Scarlett

ESTATE GROWN
FAMILY VINEYARDS

CABERNET SAU
RUTHERFORD, NA

Scarlett

COMPANY   McGah Family Cellars, Alamo, California
APPELLATION   Rutherford, Napa Valley, California

Like so many winemakers and owners, Sherratt Reicher is a
wonderful blend of perfectionist and romantic. He is not interested
in just making wines. He wants to make handcrafted, small
production, ultra-premium wines that express the best of California
Wine Country and that are elegant in structure and balance and
consistent in quality, vintage after vintage. Sherratt has the
perfect vineyard and conditions to work with: a sixty-four-acre
vineyard in the Rutherford appellation of the Napa Valley, a locale
where the days are hot, but the cool evenings extend the ripening
time. Sherratt treats his wines like rare jewels, limiting his production
to five hundred cases a year. And he named the brand after a real
jewel: his daughter, Scarlett.

When Sherratt came to us, he wanted the packaging for Scarlett
to be modern and artistic, something truly special and stylish,
while still honoring his daughter. We took our inspiration from the
warm, distinctive style of Czech painter Alphonse Mucha (1860–
1939), an art nouveau pioneer whose mural art and advertising
posters often featured lovely women with expressively flowing hair.
In the modern-day work of an European illustrator, we found
exactly the style illustration we wanted, a young woman of classic
beauty. We reworked that image into a brilliant scarlet red, then
we wove gold foil grape leaves into her flowing hair. Arresting and
exotic, the resulting label is a fairy tale vision of Sherratt's goddess
of the vineyards.

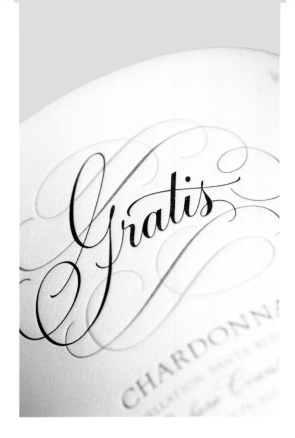

Sea Smoke

COMPANY   SEA SMOKE CELLARS, SANTA BARBARA, CALIFORNIA
APPELLATION   SANTA RITA HILLS, SANTA BARBARA, CALIFORNIA

Like many great winemakers, Bob Davids believes that the finest wines are intimate expressions of the land, soil, climate and even the spirit of where they are grown. From that point of view, Bob feels he has found a perfect place to make Burgundian-style Pinot Noirs of transcendent quality and character: an idyllic stretch of land on the western end of the Santa Rita Hills, outside Santa Barbara. On a summer's day, Bob's vineyards are bathed in sunlight and heat, but come evening, up the Santa Ynez River canyon comes a layer of rolling maritime fog, called "sea smoke," cooling the vineyard and the fruit. That sea smoke gives Bob just what he wants—the extended maturation period absolutely essential to the growing and crafting of world-class Pinot Noirs.

As a name, Sea Smoke was a natural, but Bob knew he also needed an elegant and distinctive label, something that would pay tribute to his vineyard's privileged locale and its special spirit of place. We listened carefully to Bob, studied the character and terrain of his property, and absorbed the feeling, and then we set out to create something that would be wholly unexpected and not cliché.

We created a label that discreetly evokes the feeling of sea smoke through a tantalizing, hand-drawn icon that swirls with movement and grace. We created the initial draft of the Sea Smoke wordmark, and then we took it to the master, the late Doyald Young, a king of the art of calligraphy and a man who could convey a mood or a feeling with a single flowing stroke of his pen or brush. What Doyald created is a masterpiece of calligraphy: the name Sea Smoke crafted in billowing lines and curls, a vision as mystical and alluring as Bob's sea smoke rolling up the bed of the canyon. With a similar mood, the back label was designed to slowly fade from top to bottom so that it feels as if the type is sinking into the fog—a subtle touch that seems to fall gently into the viewer's consciousness.

In a matching style, we created a sister label for Gratis, a companion Chardonnay that Bob Davids offers to his top Sea Smoke clients gratis, free of charge. This is not idle generosity; this is the spirit of the man.

SLINGSHOT

NAPA VALLEY
CABERNET SAUVIGNON

IRREVERENTLY MADE IN THE NAPA VALLEY

Slingshot

COMPANY SLINGSHOT WINES, NAPA, CALIFORNIA
APPELLATION NAPA VALLEY, CALIFORNIA

In 1999 Michael Stewart sold his Houston-based computer business and moved to the Napa Valley with the dream of making great wine. He launched Stewart Cellars and hired the celebrated consulting winemaker Paul Hobbs with the mission to create a super premium Napa Valley Cabernet Sauvignon. Soon they were off to a brilliant start.

Six years later, Michael's son, James, left a budding career in reality TV in Los Angeles and came to the Napa Valley to help his father and to learn the wine business from the ground up. Out on the road selling wine, James spotted an opportunity: use unsold grapes from his dad's vineyard to create a line of lower-priced wines aimed at youthful consumers. And so Slingshot was born. In James's eyes, this is a brand young at heart with attitude and swagger. "It's about putting your best foot forward while forgetting about fitting into the mold or following the rules," he says. "Be bold, be adventurous, choose your own path and, above all, remember to have fun."

Several years after the initial launch of Slingshot, James asked CF Napa to reenergize his brand and messaging. Finding that the original label and packaging did not match the brand's young, irreverent spirit, we developed the tagline "Irreverently made in the Napa Valley." Then, building on the refined positioning and equity of the existing slingshot logo, we found a graphic image that would dramatically convey the brand's upstart personality: a bull's-eye. The image, both familiar and impactful, was perfectly suited to take the visual lead on the label.

The resulting label design features a hole that is die-cut through the bull's-eye and the label itself, allowing the glass of the bottle to show through as if the label has been shot through by a slingshot projectile. The effect completes what is undeniably one of the more eye-catching wine label designs on the market today.

DECOY

Napa Valley

— RED WINE —

2007

Duckhorn Wine Company

LOCATION   NAPA VALLEY, CALIFORNIA

Dan Duckhorn grew up in Northern California, earned his MBA at the University of California, Berkeley, and then headed into a traditional career in business. In 1971, though, Dan became president of a vineyard management company, and suddenly a whole new world opened at his feet. Soon he was tromping through vineyards in Napa, Sonoma and France, learning about wine from the ground up. Before long, he was hooked.

In 1976, Dan and his wife, Margaret, launched their signature winery in the heart of the Napa Valley, intent on crafting beautiful varietal wines in the great Bordeaux tradition. They succeeded, brilliantly, and today Duckhorn is considered one of the leading wine producers in the whole of North America.

DECOY NAPA VALLEY

When they came to CF Napa, the folks at Duckhorn had one overriding ambition: to make their brand even more successful, while still retaining the key brand qualities that made it an icon in the first place. They also wanted to restructure their tiers of wines in a way that ended the confusion that had become prevalent at their respective target prices.

Over the years, the Duckhorns had built their brand and their image around artful renderings of ducks. Ducks were featured on many of their labels, and the work of many nature artists was also showcased in the winery's tasting room. For the Duckhorn brand, the mallard duck was definitely an equity element and so we set our sights on refreshing the icon and building on it in more effective ways.

Our first task was to redesign the company's second label, Decoy, and transform it into a widely distributed, entry-level wine brand. To do that, we made the Decoy packaging far more upscale and more commensurate with the quality promise of the other wines in the Duckhorn family. Our second task was to connect Decoy to Duckhorn, but without detracting from the higher-priced Duckhorn wines. Here we were able to leverage the beautiful painting of the mallard decoy on the existing Decoy label. The decoy was incorporated into a much more premium design, and rather than echo the Duckhorn imagery, we instead designed a special seal with the silhouettes of flying ducks— a subtle linkage to the larger Duckhorn portfolio.

PHOTO LEFT: *Decoy*

DUCKHORN VINEYARDS MAIN TIER NAPA VALLEY

Our next challenge was to end the visual confusion between the main tier and the higher-end, vineyard-designate wines. Here we had to establish two clearly different looks for the tiers, but they still needed to present a cohesive family feel.

In examining the main tier Duckhorn label, we identified its signature elements as the brand's yellow label color and its iconic mallard duck. When we looked more closely, though, we saw that the mallard was not anatomically correct

for the species, thus putting it at odds with the brand's tie to natural realism. To redress that inconsistency, we worked with a nature artist to redraw the mallard icon more accurately. Next, we created a new wordmark that stacked the brand name so that it could be enlarged in size for increased readability. We also developed a proprietary paper texture for the brand that looks like water ripples carved out of wood.

DUCKHORN VINEYARDS VINEYARD DESIGNATE TIER NAPA VALLEY

The vineyard designate tier was then designed as a larger label with a smaller duck symbol along with clearly identified vineyard information. This way at a glance, it could be easily differentiated from the main Napa Valley tier, while still remaining firmly grounded in the larger brand family.

PHOTO LEFT: *Duckhorn Vineyards Main Tier*
PHOTO RIGHT: *Duckhorn Vineyards Vineyard Designate Tier*

THE DISCUSSION NAPA VALLEY

We had one final challenge: to create an exciting, high-end package for The Discussion, Duckhorn's new Cabernet Sauvignon-based red blend. The Discussion was to be their top-of-the-line wine, the highest expression of the Duckhorn artistry, and the packaging needed to convey that—exquisitely.

The Discussion story began over three decades ago. Before crafting their very first vintage, the Duckhorns and their winemaker had a passionate discussion about what direction to follow. Should they make a cuvée—a French-style blend—or should they focus on making varietal wines? At the time, the Duckhorns chose to focus on crafting varietals like Cabernet Sauvignon. Still, Duckhorn Vineyards remained fascinated by artful blends,

and when it decided to create a proprietary cuvée as its top-tier wine, the name The Discussion naturally came to mind.

For The Discussion, we designed a rich black label and drew the duck icon to read correctly in the gold foil. To house this exceptional wine, we designed a custom box crafted from a sleek neoprene-like material debossed with the branding that has become almost as much of a collector's item as the wine itself.

PHOTO ABOVE: *The Discussion Gift Box*
PHOTO RIGHT: *Duckhorn Vineyards The Discussion*

DUCKHORN
VINEYARDS

The Discussion

NAPA VALLEY

2006 | ESTATE GROWN

Brazin

COMPANY DFV Wines, Napa, California
APPELLATION Lodi, California

As its name playfully suggests, Brazin is an audacious Old Vine
Zinfandel, with big, swaggering fruit that explodes with flavor. For
a wine this bold and brash, the Indelicato family wanted a label
that would not cower quietly on the shelf. They needed a label that
would stand up and shout, while at the same time pay homage to
the ancient, gnarled vines in Lodi that produce some of the most
distinctive Zinfandels in California.

The resulting label's central graphic is a character-rich, Old Growth
Zinfandel vine shown in silhouette and constructed from tiny,
hand-drawn renderings of the brand name, Brazin. The vine is
printed in stark contrast against the white background of the
label and is embossed, giving the vine a rich, tactile feel, as if it is
growing off of the bottle. The final, aptly brazen touch: a roughly
scrawled brand name, Brazin, is highlighted in a brilliant orange
that jumps immediately to the eye.

2008

CHARDONNAY

47% MONTEREY COUNTY
31% SAN LUIS OBISPO COUNTY
22% SANTA BARBARA COUNTY

JADE
MOUNTAIN

2008

CABERNET SAUVIGNON

55% NAPA COUNTY
41% SONOMA COUNTY
4% LAKE COUNTY

JADE
MOUNTAIN

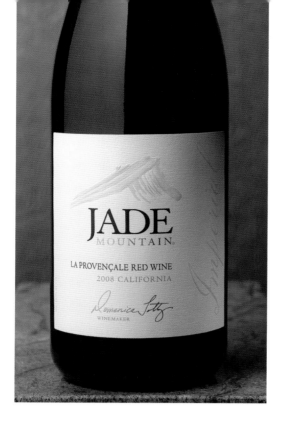

Jade Mountain Vineyards

COMPANY DIAGEO CHATEAU & ESTATE WINES, NAPA, CALIFORNIA
APPELLATION NAPA VALLEY, SONOMA COUNTY AND LAKE COUNTY, CALIFORNIA

There is a big ambition behind Jade Mountain Vineyards. Since its creation in 1988, Jade Mountain has set out to prove that if you plant top-quality California vineyards with top-quality Rhône River varietals, you can produce Rhône-style California wines that are every bit as good as the best of France and Australia. That ambition is now bearing fruit.

Jade Mountain's flagship vineyard location was the Paras Vineyard, located on the upper slopes of Mount Veeder and overlooking a magnificent expanse of the Napa Valley. With its rocky terraces and eastern exposures, the Paras Vineyard was producing Syrah and other Rhône grapes of exciting quality. From this and its other select vineyards, Jade Mountain crafted Syrah, Mourvèdre, Viognier and a proprietary southern Rhône-style blend called La Provençale.

Diageo Chateau & Estate Wines came to CF Napa to redesign and reposition its Jade Mountain brand into two tiers of wines. The new lower tier was to leverage a key asset: grapes sourced from three different appellations. This asset allows Jade Mountain to create exceptional wines without being confined to a single appellation. Above the more affordable lower tier, Diageo wanted to

create a small-lot upper tier dedicated to higher-priced wines of exceptional quality.

In search of compelling imagery for the brand, we studied the history of jade and classical Asian imagery. With these influences we used a Japanese brush to create a distinctive mountain icon using only a bold stroke or two. For the lower tier, the image was stamped in reflective silver foil and overprinted with three separate green and blue inks, giving the Jade Mountain a deep, almost iridescent look, reminiscent of high-quality jade stone. As a final touch, the Japanese brush strokes were given a sculpted emboss, making it look as if the Jade Mountain were hand-painted on each label.

For the upper tier, we created a more classic label design with both French and Asian aesthetics combined. The mountain on this tier is embossed with a glossy white foil, then overprinted with subtle gray ink to provide additional dimension and texture. The label's final touch is the signature of winemaker Domenica Totty, stamped in gold foil. Clean, simple and elegant, the label is exquisite in its simplicity. Perfect for the top of the line.

PHOTO LEFT: *Jade Mountain Main Tier*
PHOTO ABOVE: *Jade Mountain Upper Tier*

Charles Krug

COMPANY THE CHARLES KRUG WINERY, NAPA, CALIFORNIA
APPELLATION NAPA VALLEY, CALIFORNIA

The history of California wine begins right here. In the 1850s, a Prussian immigrant named Charles Krug came to California and became interested in making apple cider and wine. In 1861 at the age of only twenty-seven, Krug started his own winery–the very first in the Napa Valley. During World War II, Cesare Mondavi purchased the Charles Krug Winery, and today the winery is still owned and operated by Cesare's son, Peter Mondavi Sr., and his two sons.

Over its long history, the Charles Krug label and brand have been periodically updated, and when the family felt it was again time for a refreshed look, the Mondavis came to CF Napa. Some of their original brand assets, including a lovely historical script logo, had been allowed to deteriorate over the years. The project began by researching this seventy-five-year-old equity element to see if it could be redrawn to work across all the tiers of their product line, thus improving both its readability on the shelf and Charles Krug's brand cohesion. To that end, our design team worked closely with the late Doyald Young, a renowned calligrapher, to redraw the script, making its line weights bolder and more readable. This new script solved the problem on packaging and worked across all of Charles Krug's marketing materials and winery signage.

Down the right side of the new label we placed the debossed date, 1861, proudly saluting Charles Krug's rich heritage. In addition, the historic Charles Krug seal was refreshed and placed discreetly on the left, carrying equity over from the old labels to the new. Finally, as a completing touch, the historic claim, "Napa Valley's First Winery, Established 1861," was added. Now every bottle of Charles Krug looks fresh and contemporary, but with a timeless celebration of its privileged place in the history of American wine.

Charles Krug

PETER MONDAVI FAMILY

2004
CABERNET SAUVIGNON
NAPA VALLEY

NAPA VALLEY'S FIRST WINERY
ESTABLISHED IN 1861

redtree

CABERNET SAUVIGNON

CALIFORNIA | 20 05

Cecchetti Wine Company

Cecchetti Wine Company

LOCATION   SONOMA, CALIFORNIA

Roy Cecchetti thought he had a winner. When he launched his Redtree line back in 2007, Roy felt sure that waves of consumers would flock to his fresh, fruit-forward, distinctive varietals, especially at their attractive target price of $7 to $8.99 a bottle.

But Roy was disappointed. Soon after the launch, sales of Redtree rapidly slumped. Roy then received some disturbing feedback from his key accounts: The label and the packaging were too dark; consumers found them ominous, even frightening. Yes, the wine was cheerful and delicious, but the look and feel were anything but.

REDTREE CALIFORNIA

Filled with worry, Roy came to CF Napa looking for answers. He needed to overhaul the packaging and do it fast–he wanted to relaunch the brand as soon as possible. Otherwise, he could lose a small fortune. In response, we developed a new positioning and a new story for the brand, both based on Redtree's rural California roots. Our inspiration came from those wonderful mom-and-pop fruit stands found along so many of California's country roads. They defined for us the core personality of Redtree: fresh, high-quality, authentic and wonderful value.

The label we designed was sunny, friendly and inviting. We used a custom burlap texture on the label to create a warm, contemporary feel. Our color palette was a simple, monochromatic red, and we used it for both the red and white wines, an unconventional decision, but it helped reinforce

the brand name. In addition, the brand name, Redtree, was placed vertically along the label and debossed, providing another contemporary twist. As a final touch, we added a small, secondary label that, along with a faux historic Cecchetti Wine Company script, provided just the right touch of down-home authenticity.

The relaunch in 2008 was a massive success. Every year since, Redtree has been named the "Hot Prospect Brand" by *Impact Newsletter* and *Market Watch* magazine and the top "Growth Brand" from *Beverage Dynamics*. As of 2012, the Redtree brand was selling 142,000 cases a year and growing.

LINE 39 Lake County, North Coast and Central Coast, California

Soon after the resurrection of Redtree, Roy Cecchetti asked us to put some new energy into his Line 39 brand. The brand had a good story: the thirty-ninth parallel runs through many of the world's prime wine-growing regions, including Line 39's home vineyards in Lake County, which lies just north of the Napa Valley but does not have the high cost of Napa grapes. Overall, the soil and climate conditions in Lake County make for a winegrowing region with enormous potential. Still, Line 39 was just not performing as it should. In our eyes, the packaging was partly to blame; it did not properly communicate the quality of the wine or the underlying brand concept.

We developed a classy new logo for Line 39, one that interlocks the 3 and the 9 and extends the longitudinal "Line 39" out on both sides. From there, with Roy's approval, we tried something novel: we designed the white wines to appeal more to women and the red wines more to men. Color was the key. For the Cabernet, we used a clean, conservative black typography on a cream background. For the Sauvignon Blanc, we used a vibrant Tiffany Blue, a first for the wine industry and an instant success with female wine buyers and drinkers. Imitation being the highest form of flattery, the Tiffany Blue has since been used on scores of US wine labels.

Like Redtree, Line 39 relaunched to incredible success and won the same brand growth awards.

BACKHOUSE WINES CALIFORNIA

In 1994 Roy and Rachael Cecchetti purchased a two-and-a-half-acre parcel in the Sonoma Valley, one mile east of the famous Sonoma Plaza. On that plot, located next to a lovely willow tree and a natural, spring-fed pond, Roy and Rachel found an intriguing old backhouse. They did some research and found that the backhouse harkened back to a time when the property was a popular hangout for a variety of winemakers, writers, artists and others who craved the solitude and enjoyment of nature. Roy had started his wine company with modest resources, and that humble backhouse seemed to be an appropriate symbol of his own artistic roots and modest beginnings. And Backhouse seemed an appropriate name for a wine as well.

In keeping with that story, we developed a clean, simple cream-colored label with distinctive red lettering. In the Backhouse name, we placed a small house inside the *H*–a discreet but elegant touch. In an echo of the roof of the house, we cut a notch into the top of the label to highlight the vintage date. The resulting label is modern and sophisticated, promising a higher quality of wine than the price tag would imply.

AUSTERITY CALIFORNIA

When the US economy began to sputter, Roy Cecchetti came to CF Napa with the following brand proposition: "Create a new wine brand called Austerity that looks like a million bucks, tastes like a million bucks, but doesn't cost a million bucks." In other words, create a package design that cuts directly against the name itself. Whereas the word *austerity* implies cutting back and lowering your spending, these wines had to look and feel as if they would deliver luxurious taste at a modest price. In tough economic times, this was an alluring proposition for wine drinkers.

The Austerity brand consists of a lovely pair of red and white wine blends, attractively priced at about $14 a bottle. Our packaging solution took its inspiration from the typography of classic bank notes and historic stock certificates. The elegant hand-drawn type was then foil-stamped in gold foil along with the tagline we developed: "Wines of the Highest Discipline," promising wines of a value far beyond their affordable price tag. As a result, Austerity became a wine that consumers eagerly reach for, even when they have curbed their spending during times of fiscal austerity.

PROPRIETARY WHITE WINE

PROPRIETARY RED WINE

AUSTERITY

AUSTERITY

WINES OF THE HIGHEST DISCIPLINE

2011

2011
VINTAGE DATED

Product of California

Product of California

ALCOHOL 13.5% BY VOLUME

Landy Family Vineyards

COMPANY LANDY FAMILY VINEYARDS, HEALDSBURG, CALIFORNIA

APPELLATION RUSSIAN RIVER VALLEY, CALIFORNIA

Sometimes exploring a new road can change your life. One day Jim and Christina Landy were having an enjoyable time tasting wines in the Russian River Valley in Sonoma County with their six-week-old son, Luke, in tow. After one winery stop, the Landys found themselves driving along Sweetwater Springs Road, and then, on an impulse, they turned down a rugged dirt road. Jim and Christina fell in love with the area, and for them a whole new life was soon to begin.

The Landys bought a lovely piece of land there and launched the Landy Family Vineyards. For guidance, they turned to one of the best in the business: Paul Hobbs, a gifted winemaker who owns wineries in Sonoma County and Argentina and also consults for wineries around the world. With Hobbs's help, the Landys were soon producing exquisite Russian River wines.

The Landys asked CF Napa to create brand packaging that would feel thoroughly Californian but also contain the classic Old World cues for Pinot Noir, including a family crest. With the Landys, we explored different crests and also the folklore that surrounds griffins, those mythological creatures with the body of a lion and the head and wings of an eagle. Because the lion was traditionally considered the king of the beasts and the eagle the king of the birds, the griffin was thought to be an especially powerful and majestic creature. Griffins were also known for their courage and skill in guarding treasure and priceless possessions.

The solution we created was a historic-looking crest featuring two gilded griffins, alluding to the gold that griffins were known to guard. The griffins hold an ornate monogram made from an interlocking *L* and *V* that together form the brand's family crest. An elegant script pays tribute to the Burgundian roots of Pinot Noir and its new roots in the Russian River Valley.

Acordeón

COMPANY   FREIXENET USA, SONOMA, CALIFORNIA
APPELLATION MENDOZA, ARGENTINA

Argentina's Mendoza Province is a cultural treasure, a thriving hub of food and wine, olive oil and sophisticated tourism. It is also a region of lakes, vineyards and wildlife, all nestled in view of the imposing Andes Mountains. Argentina is today one of the global wine industry's most exciting new frontiers, and at the center is Mendoza Province. This region, with its high altitude and low humidity, produces more than 60 percent of the nation's wines, and it is known especially for its choice Malbec and Sémillon grapes and wines. Mendoza Province also has a special attribute: a natural resistance to troublesome insects, fungi and mold. As a result, Mendoza's vineyards can be cultivated as naturally as possible, facilitating the production of glorious fruit and wines.

Understandably, Mendoza Province has attracted interest and investments from many of the world's leading wineries, including Freixenet, the Spanish company with a pedigree in fine wine stretching back 150 years. Over the years, Freixenet has built a strong presence in Mendoza, and the company produces a line of bold, expressive Argentine wines marketed under the name Acordeón.

To bring new energy to its Acordeón brand, Freixenet came to CF Napa. Its previous packaging made use of a whimsical drawing of an accordion, the musical instrument so popular in Argentina's folk songs and heritage. The packaging had failed to highlight the brand or the quality of its wines. The grapes for Acordeón are grown in some of the highest viticulture elevations in the world. Most come from Finca Ferrer, a 783-acre estate located in the prestigious Tupungato region of the Uco Valley (4,167 feet) and named for the founding family of Freixenet. The winery is an example of modern architecture at its finest, and it is surrounded by terraced, high-elevation vineyards.

In our eyes, those vineyards were nature's version of the folds of an accordion, and this led to a new icon for the brand. We started with an abstract capital letter *A*, like a mountain, and then we intersected that *A* with a bold graphic representation of those elevated vineyard rows. That was it: stark, modern, New World and most importantly, very high-end. These wines from Argentina are of exceptional quality, and now they have a presentation to match.

2008

FORCE
Majeure

CIEL DU CHEVAL VINEYARD
RED MOUNTAIN

COLLABORATION SERIES I
RED WINE

Force Majeure

COMPANY   FORCE MAJEURE VINEYARDS, RED MOUNTAIN, WASHINGTON

APPELLATION   RED MOUNTAIN, WASHINGTON

When the California businessman Paul McBride first moved to Washington State back in 1994, he was dismissive of Washington's wines. In his mind, Napa, Sonoma, Oregon–that was Wine Country, not rainy Washington State. But then McBride tasted some of the best wines in the region, and he realized that Washington State had the potential to become a world-class wine producer. McBride began looking for a place to create a winery of his own. And soon he found it: Red Mountain, located southeast of Seattle and Yakima. Thus was born Force Majeure, a joint effort of McBride and Ryan Johnson, a gifted vineyard manager in the region. Together, McBride and Johnson set out to produce vineyard-designated, limited-quantity wines, and soon the critics began to hail their results. McBride and Johnson were off and running.

When they turned to us for help with design for their new brand, we knew that subtlety was out. To promote a brand like Force Majeure, we needed power and strength. On the packaging, we used a dramatic black backdrop to frame a large, extravagant wordmark in silver and white. The main graphic features a set of stylized wings taking flight; the wings framing a heraldic crest with the initials *F* and *M* etched inside. Each wine was then given a series number, similar to a limited-edition piece of artwork, thus highlighting the exquisite boutique nature of the wine inside.

Epica

COMPANY   VIÑA SAN PEDRO WINE GROUP, SANTIAGO, CHILE
APPELLATION   CHILE

In the eyes of many wine consumers, Chile is viewed as a New World wine region, but in truth, Chile has produced fine wines since the sixteenth century. That was when Spanish conquistadors brought to Chile cuttings of *Vitis vinifera,* the traditional species of European grapes. By the mid-nineteenth century, French varietals such as Cabernet Sauvignon and Merlot had been planted in this vibrant South American nation, producing some very fine wines. The modern era of winemaking in Chile is proving to be even more exciting, with several innovative companies leading the way. Still, most Chilean brands remain largely unknown in the US.

Viña San Pedro, among Chile's most respected and largest wine producers, was determined to change that. In 2010 it came to CF Napa with plans to launch an ambitious new wine brand custom-tailored for the US market. After witnessing the breakthrough success of our other brands, it wanted to score a similar triumph for Chilean wine. As a starting point, Viña San Pedro asked us to assess US consumers' perceptions of Chile and then identify the correct demographic for it to target, as well as the ideal price for wine consumers.

Our research was revealing. We found that the best marketing demographic would be the so-called millennials, the generation that came of age with the turn of the millennium. And we determined that for them the optimal price would be approximately $10 a bottle. Further, after our testing showed that these wine consumers viewed Chile as natural and exotic, we concluded that we should position the new wine as an exciting new "discovery brand." On that foundation, and working closely with market testing specialists, we then developed two or three potential names and positioning messages for the new Chilean wine brand. The clear brand name winner was Epica, a Spanish word that translates easily into English as "epic," a term often used by millennials to describe something as amazing, even life-transforming. That word embodied a compelling message: Live big. Epica is about possibilities. It is about seeing the potential in any moment and celebrating the magic in it.

To convey that message in the design, the brand name, Epica, is positioned large and vertically on the label, with the final *A* standing upright. This way the *A* subtly evokes the Andes Mountains and helps consumers read the brand name as EPIC. To differentiate the varietals, we placed a colored foil dot corresponding to the flavor of its given varietal on the *I* of the EPICA wordmark. As a final touch, we created a custom lineal pattern that is debossed into the label to give the entire package a modern cartographic feel that invites the consumer to discover these exciting wines.

EPICA

WINE OF | 2010
CHILE | CABERNET
SAUVIGNON

SAN PEDRO

DOUBLE CANYON

HORSE HEAVEN HILLS
CABERNET SAUVIGNON

2010

DOUBLE CANYON VINEYARD

Double Canyon

COMPANY CRIMSON WINE GROUP, NAPA, CALIFORNIA
APPELLATION HORSE HEAVEN HILLS, WASHINGTON STATE

Horse Heaven Hills is located in a remote corner of Washington State and borders the Yakima Valley appellation on the north and the Columbia River on the south. The appellation is distinguished by the strong western winds that roll through the Columbia Gorge and reduce the likelihood of rot and fungal diseases. With few estate wineries in the area, the region–home to many prestigious, award-winning wines–has remained a well-kept secret for decades.

The Crimson Wine Group saw the potential of Horse Heaven Hills, and in 2007 they found the perfect property on which to grow an authentic estate-grown wine. They named it Double Canyon. One of only five estates in the Horse Heaven Hills appellation, Double Canyon takes its name from the two ravines that run through its vineyard.

For this packaging project, we first explored ways to convey those two canyons in their vineyard, but ultimately our focus shifted to the region's unique micro-climate, which is so crucial to the quality of Double Canyon's grapes. To evoke those beneficial winds, we drew abstract undulating lines and flowed them across a field of metallic silver. Additionally, these lines were printed in a pearl white tactile silkscreen to create a rich texture. The result is a contemporary label conveying the vastness of the terroir and those winds, making for a label that is as visually arresting as it is pleasing to the touch.

Fetzer Vineyards

LOCATION MENDOCINO COUNTY, CALIFORNIA

Barney Fetzer was a true visionary. Over fifty years ago, Barney and his family chose to settle in beautiful Mendocino County and devote their lives not just to making fine wine but also to preserving the land and keeping it pristine for generations to come. At that time, being environmentally conscious was not viewed as accepted wisdom; it was seen as little more than a passing fad. Barney Fetzer helped change all that.

From his base in Mendocino, Barney built Fetzer into a household name. Then, in 1992 the Fetzer family sold the business to Brown-Forman, the Kentucky-based beverage giant and producer of Jack Daniels Tennessee Whiskey. In 2009 CF Napa began working with Brown-Forman to reposition the brand and recapture its past position as a market leader. We began by studying the history of the Fetzer family and Barney Fetzer's philosophy. From this, we built the Fetzer brand's story and then distilled it down to a succinct brand essence that supported its tagline "The Earth Friendly Winery."

FETZER VINEYARDS CALIFORNIA

Then in 2011 Fetzer was sold again, this time to Viña Concha y Toro S.A., Chile's preeminent wine producer. Given our experience with the brand and our vision for its future, Concha y Toro kept us aboard. From there, we focused on Fetzer's core brand, and we redesigned the packaging to be more premium, refreshed and engaging. The main illustration of the historic Valley Oaks property was refurbished and presented in bright, fresh colors, providing flavor cues for the corresponding wines. Rich embossing and gold foil were added to the label to give it a luxurious feel, while each label proudly cites a different aspect of Fetzer's commitment to sustainability. One statement, for instance, says, "Winery operations powered by 100% green energy." These claims are all true– and perfectly attuned to today's young, socially and environmentally conscious wine consumer.

PHOTO RIGHT: *Fetzer Vineyards*

FETZER
THE EARTH FRIENDLY WINERY
Valley Oaks
CABERNET SAUVIGNON
CALIFORNIA
2008
PIONEERS IN SUSTAINABILITY
SINCE 1986
14% LESS CARBON EMISSIONS
FETZER
Valley Oaks
CHARDONNAY

FETZER MENDO MENDOCINO COUNTY

From there, we helped create two new extensions to the Fetzer
brand. The first was Fetzer Mendo, a brand that celebrates the
Fetzer's Mendocino County and rural California roots and its
commitment to sustainable farming. The label features an
illustration of the picturesque California Coast and its revered
giant Sequoia trees, created using torn paper and an ink brush
effect to convey the appropriate rustic feel.

FETZER CRIMSON AND QUARTZ CALIFORNIA

The second brand extension was a new pair of Fetzer red and white wine blends, Crimson and Quartz. These celebrate the Fetzer brand's natural, carefree–some might say "hippie"–personality. In line with Fetzer's boutique, handcrafted spirit, we hand-drew the entire label, including all the type. The style of the labels simulates the layered look of a silk-screened label, accentuated even further by multiple layers of embossing. Crimson and Quartz now stand out beautifully on the shelf and have proven so popular that the brand has grown into a full line of wines.

PHOTO LEFT: *Fetzer Mendo*
PHOTO RIGHT: *Fetzer Crimson and Quartz*

JOHN ANTHONY

2003
NAPA VALLEY
CABERNET SAUVIGNON

John Anthony

COMPANY   JOHN ANTHONY VINEYARDS, NAPA, CALIFORNIA
APPELLATION   NAPA VALLEY, CALIFORNIA

John Anthony Truchard grew up on his father's winery in the Carneros District of the Napa Valley. As a boy, John played in the vineyard, brushed dirt from his knees, and picked grape skins from his fingernails. In his mind, he was destined to one day make handcrafted wines from some of the best fruit produced in the Napa Valley. And from the beginning, John knew he would do it differently. Gone were the days of purchasing a large estate, building a winery and planting vines. Instead, he planned to lease choice vineyard land, carefully evaluate its soils and microclimates, and then plant only those varietals that would thrive in those locales.

With John Anthony Vineyards, John and his wife, Michele, have achieved that dream. They make beautiful wines, sourced from small vineyards, and they showcase their wines in their downtown Napa tasting lounge. No major investment in brick and mortar, just in creativity and flair. When John began his own venture, he approached CF Napa with a well-defined goal: to appeal to today's young, affluent and more discerning wine connoisseurs–and to do so in a fresh, original way.

At CF Napa, we believe the best wine labels engage multiple senses, and one underappreciated sensory component is touch. Our label for John Anthony Vineyards is a wonderful case-in-point. In our exploration for the right balance, we broke down the typography of the brand name into subtly overlapping translucent letterforms to create an organic collage. Reminiscent in shape to a grape vine, the look is both modern and iconic. To create a tactile, luxurious feel we debossed the letterforms into a rich, felt-textured paper. The result is a wine you love to taste–and a label you love to touch.

Ehlers Estate 1886

COMPANY   EHLERS ESTATE, ST. HELENA, CALIFORNIA
APPELLATION   NAPA VALLEY, CALIFORNIA

In 1985 a French entrepreneur and philanthropist named Jean Leducq began acquiring small parcels of vineyard land in the Napa Valley's acclaimed St. Helena appellation. A dedicated vintner and wine lover, Leducq envisioned building a Napa Valley estate devoted to crafting bold wines with the sophistication found in the wines of the great Bordeaux châteaus.

In 2001 Leducq added a real jewel to his collection of properties: a historic stone winery built in 1886 by the Napa Valley vintner Bernard Ehlers. The winery came with forty-three acres of outstanding vineyard. Leducq and his wife, Sylviane, revived the original Ehlers Estate name with their inaugural 2000 vintage. Jean Leducq was a man of noble spirit. When he passed away in 2002, he left the Ehlers Estate in trust to the nonprofit Leducq Foundation, which he and his wife had created in 1996 to support cardiovascular research. Today, all the proceeds from the sale of Ehlers Estate's wines go to support their foundation.

Ehlers Estate came to CF Napa with a challenge: While its wines had historically been of wonderful quality, their packaging had more of a French sensibility and no connection to the estate or its philanthropic mission. Our solution was to create a distinctive icon in the shape of a capital E. Inside that E is a small, almost hidden heart symbol. That little heart inextricably ties the Ehlers Estate to the foundation's cardiovascular research. For the Ehlers Estate's top-of-the-line Cabernet Sauvignon, we selected the name 1886, derived from the construction date chiseled on a stone plaque found on their historic estate.

For this exceptional wine, the Ehlers Estate wanted a custom glass bottle that paid homage to the winery's French heritage, so we designed the Bordeaux-shaped bottle with broad but sloped shoulders, similar to bottles from the Rhône River Valley. The bottle has a substantial taper that runs to a pronounced foot. The pièce de résistance is a stunning finish on the neck of the bottle and the use of a pewter neck wrap and top dot over the cork. The resulting package is a sleek and contemporary tribute to the best of France—and to the guiding spirit of Jean Leducq.

Aiken

COMPANY AIKEN WINES, ST. HELENA, CALIFORNIA

APPELLATION SONOMA MOUNTAIN, SONOMA, CALIFORNIA

Joel Aiken has been an internationally respected winemaker in the Napa Valley for nearly thirty years. A California native, Joel received his master's degree in enology from the esteemed wine program at the University of California, Davis, before commencing his career in the Napa Valley at the Beaulieu Vineyard (BV). Beginning as assistant winemaker in 1982, Joel ultimately became vice president of winemaking. In that capacity, he oversaw the crafting of many of BV's most distinguished wines, including its iconic Georges de Latour Cabernet Sauvignon.

When Joel "retired," he decided he wanted to start his own wine brand and asked CF Napa to help build the look and feel for his signature wines. He wanted a label that would convey luxury and elegance but do so in a way that evoked more of his own modern design sensibilities.

The result is a label of elegant simplicity, with two lines, one bold in shimmering black foil that appears to cut through to the glass bottle, the other a dashed line evocative of topographic maps, rising to the top, in perfect harmony with the *A* in Aiken. The lines suggest an ascent to the peak, conveying a feeling of elevation, in tribute to both the quality of the wines and the lush mountainside vineyards where some were born. At the foot of those lines are the precise latitudinal and longitudinal coordinates of Joel's vineyards. As a finishing touch, Joel's signature is stamped into the label. To complete the concept, the back label includes this defining tagline: "The art of wine/Elevated."

Entwine

COMPANY WENTE VINEYARDS, LIVERMORE, CALIFORNIA, IN PARTNERSHIP WITH
FOOD NETWORK, NEW YORK, NEW YORK

APPELLATION CALIFORNIA

In 2011 California's Wente Vineyards and Food Network formed a groundbreaking partnership. Their aim was to produce a line of wines that would be delicious on their own but also perfectly suited to pairing with and enhancing the flavors of food. In developing these signature wines, Food Network's expert culinary team worked hand-in-hand with winemaker Karl Wente, who represents the fifth generation of Wente family winemakers.

To create a proper foundation for this new brand, CF Napa participated in extensive consumer testing conducted by the partnership's research company, with the aim of identifying the elements of design and packaging that would best capture the brand's essence. During the process, CF Napa produced dozens of brand concepts, several of which were then tested with consumers. For CF Napa, one of the biggest challenges, beyond developing the

brand icon and packaging, was to find the best way to incorporate the Food Network and Wente Vineyards brands into one cohesive expression and story.

Our solution presents Entwine in a friendly, hand-drawn wordmark paired with vibrant flavor colors, conveying the coming together of food and wine and the friendly accessibility of the wines. The wordmark was debossed into a rich textured paper, so when the bottles are displayed side by side, the Entwine wordmark visually entwines the group. The front labels highlight the brand's founding partnership, while each of the back labels describes the wines' flavors with suggested food pairings. The Entwine line has proved to be a winning collaboration and is eagerly promoted with playful headlines like "Where Flavors Meet" and "Hello, My Name is Delicious."

entwine

CALIFORNIA

CABERNET SAUVIGNON | 2009

entwine. We teamed up with our favorite winemaking
region's wines that are great sipped on their own
and paired with food. Enjoy!

entwine

RUGBY & WINE

HOOKER

FINE ✦ WINE

RUGBY CLUB

FOOTBALL

Old Boys

CABERNET SAUVIGNON

NAPA VALLEY

VINT. **2** DATE
009

PRODUCED AND BOTTLED BY
LAWER FAMILY WINERY, ST. HELENA, CA.

RUGBY & WINE

HOOKER

RUGBY CLUB

Bonburay

CHARDONNAY

NAPA VALLEY

2

PRODUCED AND BOTTLED BY
LAWER FAMILY WINERY, NAPA, CA.

Lawer Family Wines

LOCATION CALISTOGA, CALIFORNIA

Betsy and David Lawer bring something unusual to the American wine industry: the spirit of Alaska. Betsy's family has been in banking in Anchorage for three generations, and today she serves as the vice chair of the First National Bank, Alaska. Her husband, David, a lawyer, has served as the bank's counsel for the past twenty-five years. But what really drives the Lawers is their devotion to family, duck hunting, rugby, gold mining and the art of making fine California wines.

Of these passions, wine is the newest. To have a respite from those bitter cold Alaskan winters, Betsy and David used to make annual holiday visits to California, and they particularly enjoyed poking around the Napa and Sonoma valleys, tasting wines and enjoying the fabulous food. Before long, the Lawers got hooked. In 1995, with a group of other investors, Betsy and David became part owners of the formerly defunct Folie à Deux Winery, in the northern section of the Napa Valley, up near the town of Calistoga. Soon, though, they decided to go out on their own, and in 2002 the Lawers purchased a lovely sixty-acre property just outside Calistoga. That has now been expanded into 109 acres of prime California wine country. The result is Lawer Family Wines, with Betsy, David and their daughter, Sarah, guiding the family's exciting new venture.

HOOKER RFC WINES NAPA AND SONOMA VALLEYS, CALIFORNIA

Once they had their own winery, Betsy and David turned to their other passions as inspiration for their brands. Rugby was one of these. When Betsy was growing up, her dad sang her lullabies at bedtime. The problem was, he did not know any of the traditional ones, so he improvised, playing off many of the lively and risqué songs he had learned while playing the hooker position on the Stanford University Rugby Club–leaving out the bawdy parts, of course. Betsy loved those improvised lullabies and those special times with her dad, and so it was only fitting that years later, while studying at Duke University, Betsy again had her heart swept away by another hooker, this one playing on the Duke rugby team. Yes, that was David, once again fusing love and rugby in Betsy's heart.

For the label and packaging of the Hooker wines, we sought to capture the storied tradition and spirit of rugby. The role of the hooker in rugby is to start the play by passing the ball to a teammate or by running with it. So the hooker has to be smart, adaptable and bold. We tried to convey these admirable attributes in the label. Inspired by the crests and jerseys of the world's famed rugby clubs, the crest features a lion and a bull, the astrological signs of Betsy and David. The numeral 2 in the vintage date on the label is displayed larger, providing a subtle nod to the jersey number traditionally worn by the hooker.

THREE COINS NAPA VALLEY AND SONOMA COUNTY, CALIFORNIA

Betsy Lawer's father was a savvy gold miner with a profitable claim in the foothills of Alaska's Mount McKinley. According to family lore, he had a particular method for quality control.

When mining a new area, he would select three coins and record their dates on a scrap of paper. He would then toss those coins down the hill he planned to mine. If those three coins were not at the bottom of the sluice box at clean-up time, it meant the water pressure had been too high and the coins had been washed into the tailing pile–along with some lost gold. But if they found those three coins then the job was well done, and that was as rewarding as finding any gold nugget. As the Lawers explain, "Those three coins symbolize the hard work, attention to detail and dedication it takes to do any job right. Today, we honor those same values when making our wines to celebrate the special moments in life when you 'strike gold.'"

To capture this family story we created an icon of three gold coins. Each coin is also laden with additional meaning. One features the California state bear, symbolizing the Lawers' California winery. It also references David's nickname when he played rugby. A second coin features a miner panning for gold, recalling Betsy's father and his dream of gold mining. The third coin features a woman, a tribute to Betsy, her four sisters and her daughter.

To achieve the richest possible effect, the coins are created in metallic foil with a sculptured emboss and over-printed with a rich patina to give them a look and feel that simulates that of actual coins. The finishing touch is an elegant wordmark on a richly embossed, lineal textured background, lending the label a historic monetary feel. We also added a small die-cut tab that notes the limited production of each wine, giving every bottle the exclusivity of a limited minting.

DUCK SHACK NAPA VALLEY AND SONOMA COUNTY, CALIFORNIA

The Lawer family's duck shack was a rustic retreat and a place of high adventure, camaraderie and good cheer. The food tasted better, the stars shone brighter, and the banter was always warm and lively. The duck shack will forever produce memories of crisp fall days, deep blue skies and golden grass waving in the breeze, all in the shadow of the majestic mountains towering in the distance. What better way to honor this tradition and pastime than with a line of fine wines?

To capture the spirit of this very special place for the Lawer family, we started with an iconic photograph of a duck shack, complete with ducks flying overhead. For added feeling, we gave the photo a rich sepia tone. The family's story is told in part in a handsome gold script, providing a rich

layering to the label. As a final touch, we added a monogram inspired by the historic logos of classic American gun manufacturers. If you let your mind wander in the label, you can almost smell the fresh air, feel the kick of the shotgun against your shoulder and hear the satisfying pop of that celebratory cork.

ESTABLISHED
1876
NAPA VALLEY

BERINGER.

NAPA VALLEY

CABERNET SAUVIGNON

2002

Beringer

COMPANY TREASURY WINE ESTATES, NAPA, CALIFORNIA

APPELLATION NAPA VALLEY, CALIFORNIA

Few wineries in the US have a history as long and rich as Beringer Vineyards. Located in the heart of the Napa Valley, just north of the town of St. Helena, Beringer was founded in 1875 by Jacob and Frederick Beringer, two immigrant brothers from Mainz, a winegrowing region in Germany. The brothers released their first vintage in 1876, and soon they established themselves as one of the "Big Five" powerhouses in California wine.

Over the years, like many brands, Beringer's leadership position had slipped, and in 2004 CF Napa was asked to find a way to reposition the brand to appeal to young, cosmopolitan wine consumers and to conform with the latest trends in wine packaging and branding. The challenge here was twofold: modernize the brand without alienating Beringer's long-standing clientele, and at the same time enhance the core equity in the Beringer brand, namely its rich heritage in the Napa Valley.

The solution features a fresh, modern look with elements that emphasize Beringer's distinguished history in the Napa Valley. In fact, the appellation is on the label in three different iterations, yet without feeling redundant. The primary graphic is a hand-drawn Napa Valley type that is debossed and foil-stamped into the textured label, creating a rich, modern graphic that proudly heralds its Napa Valley heritage. The phrase "Established in 1876" was highlighted, emphasizing Beringer's more than 135 years as one of Napa Valley's premier wineries. The label proved to be a huge success, elegantly reconnecting Beringer to its illustrious Napa Valley roots and setting the stage for the brand into the future.

Santa Margherita

COMPANY   TERLATO WINES INTERNATIONAL, LAKE BLUFF, ILLINOIS
AND SANTA MARGHERITA, PORTOGRUARO, ITALY

APPELLATION   ALTO ADIGE, ITALY

For many wine drinkers, the brand name Santa Margherita is almost synonymous with Pinot Grigio of the highest quality. The wines themselves, from the Alto Adige area of northeastern Italy, have a fresh, clean fragrance and crisp, layered flavors. Santa Margherita's Pinot Grigio was first launched in the United States in 1979, and more than three decades later it remains a favorite with consumers and fine restaurants. Over the years, though, as the popularity of Pinot Grigio has grown and other labels have come into the segment, the Santa Margherita brand needed refreshing. And there was an added problem: in recent years, the Pinot Grigio market segment has been hurt by wine coming in from unauthorized distributors and even plainly counterfeit sources.

CF Napa was brought in to address these concerns. Working closely with Santa Margherita and its exclusive US importer, Terlato Wines International, we reworked the hierarchy of the packaging to make it feel more consistent and familiar to US consumers and to highlight the Santa Margherita brand name first in the hierarchy rather than Pinot Grigio. We also redrew the brand's historic wordmark to make it more readable and impactful on the label. The premium appellation of Alto Adige was given more prominence next to the official Italian seal of authentication, called the *Demominazione di Origine Controllata*. That certifies the quality and origin of the bottle's contents. The border system on the original label had proved difficult to replicate consistently, so we redrew the entire border system and the imagery of the winery's historic chateau, thus opening up the artwork and facilitating the production process. The result is packaging that restores Santa Margherita to its original glory.

Santa Margherita

Pinot Grigio

2006

ALTO ADIGE

DENOMINAZIONE DI ORIGINE CONTROLLATA

PRODUCT  OF ITALY

The Black Dog Series

COMPANY   HILL WINE COMPANY, ST. HELENA, CALIFORNIA
APPELLATION   NAPA VALLEY, CALIFORNIA

Jeff Hill and his wife, Rebecca, are fervent practitioners of
sustainability and organic grape growing. After many years of
managing high-end vineyards in Napa and Sonoma counties,
in 2008 Jeff and Rebecca created the Hill Wine Company with
the aim of bringing consumers high-quality, sustainably grown
wines at a reasonable price. They use recycled glass in their
bottles, recycled paper for their labels and boxes, and corks
sourced from organically certified forests. All of Hill's company
apparel uses organic cottons and bamboo. Additionally, in line
with their love of animals and their own dog in particular, Jeff and
Rebecca launched a line of wines called the Black Dog Series,
with a percentage from every bottle sold going to the American
Society for the Prevention of Cruelty to Animals (ASPCA).

The label we created for them celebrates the character and lineage
of Labrador retrievers by highlighting one of their favorite
pursuits: hunting. The Lab is illustrated in subtle silhouette,
"pointing" in tall grass–a classic hunting pose. The bright red
Hill icon has a fresh, contemporary look and gives the Jeff Hill
group a consistent iconography that has the flexibility to work
across each of its business segments. Jeff's signature and the
limited-case production designation provide the final touch to this
modern, yet artisanal wine brand.

Alexander Valley Vineyards

COMPANY   ALEXANDER VALLEY VINEYARDS, HEALDSBURG, CALIFORNIA

APPELLATION   ALEXANDER VALLEY, CALIFORNIA

California wine owes a lot to an intrepid adventurer named Cyrus Alexander. In his early years, Alexander worked as a hunter and a trapper, and later he would pan for gold. But in 1840, at the behest of a wealthy benefactor, Alexander left San Diego on horseback and made his way north to the upper reaches of Sonoma County. His mission was to find for his benefactor a wealth of unclaimed land suitable for ranching.

What Alexander found was as good as gold: forty-eight thousand acres of unclaimed land, with excellent soil, a temperate climate and plenty of available water and timber. The lion's share of that natural wealth went to his backer, but as part of the deal Alexander kept one of the choicest parcels for himself, a grand property on the eastern side of the Russian River. From that outpost, Cyrus Alexander made his mark: that entire stretch of Sonoma County is now called Alexander Valley.

In 1962 Maggie and Harry Wetzel purchased most of Cyrus Alexander's original homestead. They started growing grapes in 1963, and in 1975, their son, Hank, produced the first vintage at the bonded winery under the label Alexander Valley Vineyards. Like many historic brands, their label and package had valuable equity elements and a high level of consumer recognition. But their packaging needed a refresh.

Their *AVV* monogram logo was redesigned to read more elegantly and cleanly, and we placed it more prominently in the center of the label to make the brand more easily identifiable at a distance and quicker to scan for in a retail environment. The wordmark was redesigned so that it too read more effortlessly, with the lengthy name no longer wrapping around the edges of the label. To give the brand an artisanal feel, we organized the appellation, the Wetzel family name and the relevant wine information at the bottom of the label in a type stack that feels more historic. The label now clearly identifies the brand as family owned and operated. The result is a respectful renovation of their previous label that modernizes it for today's wine market.

ALEXANDER VALLEY VINEYARDS

CABERNET SAUVIGNON

ALEXANDER VALLEY

Estate Grown & Bottled

SONOMA COUNTY   Vintage 2010

ESTABLISHED 1962   WETZEL FAMILY ESTATE

Caraccioli Cellars

COMPANY   CARACCIOLI CELLARS, CARMEL, CALIFORNIA
APPELLATION   SANTA LUCIA HIGHLANDS, CALIFORNIA

Gary Caraccioli is a man of the earth. He and his brother, Phil, grew up working on their family's farm in the valley at the foot of the Santa Lucia Mountains. As kids, Gary and Phil spent many hours watching their grandfather pour his love into making homemade wines, just as his family had done for generations in the Italian-speaking portion of Switzerland. For the Caracciolis, enjoying wine was not a luxury confined to fancy bistros or wine bars; it was an absolutely essential part of the pleasures and bonding of the family table.

In 2006 Gary and the Caraccioli family launched a new venture: making their own sparkling and still wines at their lovely mountainside property in the Santa Lucia Highlands. Asking CF Napa to help them launch their new brand, they sought a distinctive look that would be at once elegant and modern.

The result is a sleek black package influenced by the high fashion of Italy and brands like Gucci and Prada. The labels feature a custom-debossed pattern constructed from the letter C that creates a rich and luxuriously subtle texture. A double C icon combines with a custom-drawn script for the brand name, Caraccioli, to form the signature iconography for Caraccioli Cellars. The labels for the sparkling wines have an appealing die-cut that wraps around nearly the entire bottle and meets on the face of the package, leaving a gap between the labels that echoes the double C of the winery's namesake. The final touch is a ribbon with a small seal, creating a final "jewel" on the neck of the bottle.

PHOTO LEFT: *Caraccioli Sparkling Wines*
PHOTO ABOVE: *Caraccioli Pinot Noir*

Hahn Family Wines

LOCATION Napa, California

Nicky Hahn is a man on a mission. In the 1970s, the Swiss-born winemaker and entrepreneur fell in love with the Santa Lucia Highlands, a stretch of the Monterey Coast that has a unique climate, soil and guiding spirit. Nicky then set out to make the Santa Lucia Highlands into one of the premier winegrowing regions of California, and in 1988 he led the campaign to make the region a formal appellation. Nicky's Hahn Estates now owns 650 Santa Lucia Highlands vineyard acres, and his wines epitomize the best of the appellation.

Hahn SLH (Santa Lucia Highlands) Santa Lucia Highlands, California

For a logo, Nicky did not have far to look. In German, the family name Hahn means "rooster," and when he started out, an oil painting of a rooster provided Nicky with the umbrella logo for his brands. Over time, though, the Hahn logo and packaging had become stale, and that painting proved difficult to use across the company's multitude of branded communications. Hahn Family Wines came to CF Napa and asked us to design the packaging for its new Santa Lucia Highlands tier of wines named SLH, and ultimately, for the entire Hahn brand. Our immediate challenge was to create a fresh rooster that would be immediately recognizable, but we also felt it was essential to sidestep what was then a growing craze for wine labels featuring more whimsical expressions of animals.

In pursuit of the right imagery, we drew hundreds of roosters and rooster-inspired logo marks. Ultimately, we found our solution using a Japanese brush that provided both the texture and feeling of freedom that we wanted to communicate. The color for the brand was a natural. It had to be red, symbolic of the rooster's red crown–and also an excellent color for shelf visibility. From there, the SLH label was printed on a rich textured paper, with each vintage written in a series of dots laser die-cut through the label, exposing the glint of the glass bottle behind it. For Hahn SLH, the result is luxurious, yet distinctly New World and iconic.

Déjà Vu California

Déjà Vu is a line of Hahn Family Wines that was developed specifically for the European market and sensibility. The aim for the brand was to be conservative and premium in nature and thus appropriate for the European consumer, but without being boring or stuffy. With a target consumer who wanted a value-priced wine that still promised higher quality, the packaging would need to jump off the shelf, without being too trendy or brash.

Our solution evokes the eerie, foggy sensation that comes when we are struck by a sense of déjà vu. Seen from a distance, the label appears quite traditional, with the wordmark reading boldly in red and black and the remaining typography set unobtrusively at the bottom of the label. However, as consumers approach the bottle, they see something else: The brand name is repeated upside down and presented in clear, pearlescent foil. This creates a subtle echo of the name Déjà Vu and slyly hints that these wines have hidden assets far more seductive than their stodgy competitors.

LUCIENNE SANTA LUCIA HIGHLANDS, CALIFORNIA

Lucienne is an exquisite Pinot Noir made from fruit grown in three estate vineyards–Smith, Lone Oak and Doctor's Vineyards–located in Nicky Hahn's beloved Santa Lucia Highlands. So special is the wine that Nicky created a boutique winery within his larger winery just to make sure that Lucienne gets the loving, handcrafted attention it deserves. The result is a wine that truly expresses Nicky's own personal taste and spirit; he even named it after his middle name, Lucien, which derives from *lux*, the Latin word for "light."

There is also a double layer of meaning here: Santa Lucia, for whom these highlands were named,

was known as the Patron Saint of Light. According to ancient lore, during the yuletide and winter solstice, Santa Lucia would appear in a lovely crown of candles, thus bringing the gift of light to the winter darkness. That led us to Lucienne's guiding imagery: a stately crown of candles. To give the crown the proper look and feel, we embellished it with gold foil. The iconic crown now sits atop humble type, gently evoking the classical qualities and sensibilities of the wine's Burgundian roots. As a finishing touch, we used a white pearl foil on the border of the label, alluding to a satin-finished detail of Santa Lucia's garments.

SMITH & HOOK PASO ROBLES, CALIFORNIA

The wine industry is rich in romance and style, but it also comes loaded with uncertainty and sometimes years of trial.

In 1980 Nicky Hahn and his wife, Gaby, purchased the Smith Ranch, a lovely horse property, and the adjoining Hook Ranch, where cattle had grazed for generations. The properties were already planted with Cabernet Sauvignon grapes, and Hahn Family Wines soon launched their first signature Cabernet Sauvignon to critical acclaim. Over the years, however, the Hahn family came to the conclusion that their Santa Lucia Highlands vineyards were better suited for growing Pinot Noir, and that Smith & Hook Cabernet Sauvignon should instead be sourced from their vineyards in Paso Robles, an area known for its exceptional Bordeaux varietals.

The move has paid off handsomely. The quality of Hahn's Signature Cabernet Sauvignon is exceptional, and Hahn now has over 350 acres in the Santa Lucia Highlands planted with top-quality Pinot Noir grapes producing exquisite wines.

Hahn came to CF Napa to create a new package for Smith & Hook that would highlight the quality of their revitalized Smith & Hook Cabernet Sauvignon and the pioneering spirit of the Hahn Family Wines. We drew our inspiration from the traditional cattle ranches of the American West, and more specifically, from the simple, evocative monograms and symbols that were branded onto the sides of cattle to show ownership. We developed a proprietary monogram using the *S* and *H* from Smith & Hook and embellished it with imagery of saddles and guns from the Old West. As a final touch, it seemed appropriate that instead of paper the label would be forged out of metal and applied directly onto the bottle to proudly and distinctively "brand" every bottle as Smith & Hook.

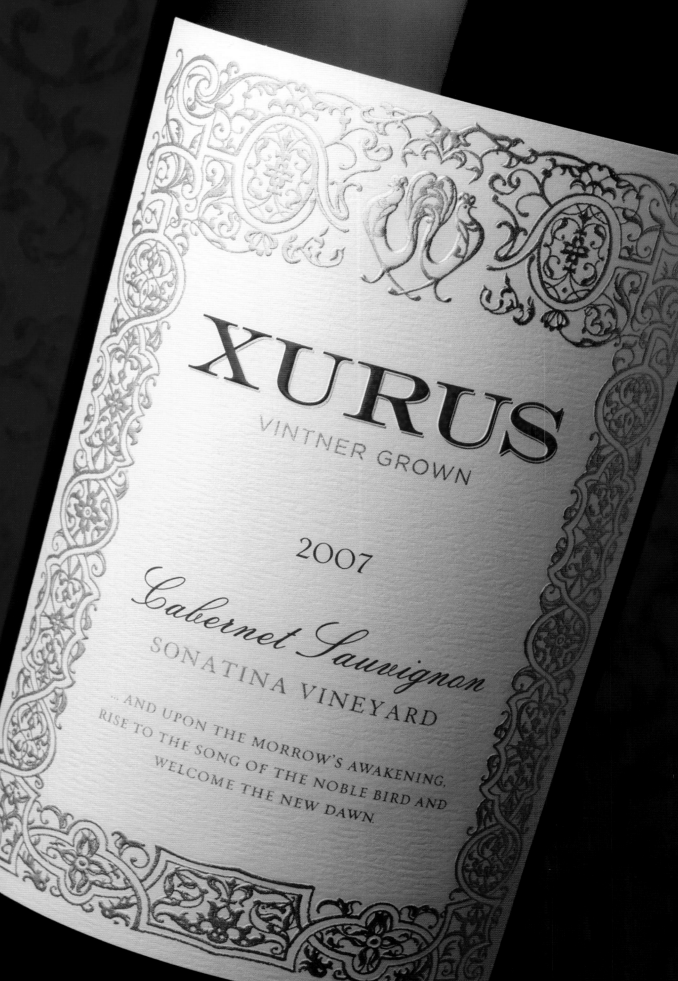

XURUS

VINTNER GROWN

2007

Cabernet Sauvignon

SONATINA VINEYARD

... AND UPON THE MORROW'S AWAKENING,
RISE TO THE SONG OF THE NOBLE BIRD AND
WELCOME THE NEW DAWN.

Xurus

COMPANY   SANAM LLC, CORTE MADERA, CALIFORNIA
APPELLATION   LAKE COUNTY, CALIFORNIA

In 1998 two businessmen originally from Persia came to the California wine country looking for a place to make fine wine and to do so in an inspiring way. Ali Namdar and Kambiz Safinya found what they were looking for in Lake County, California, just north of the Napa Valley. There they bought the Sonatina Vineyard, specifically for its exceptional Cabernet Sauvignon potential, and they set out to create a wine and a brand that would celebrate the history of wine, which traces back to their native Persia, and the elegance, art, culture and joie de vivre that wine represents.

To make their wines, Ali and Kambiz–who are brothers-in-law as well as business partners–turned to two exceptional winemakers: Denis Malbec and his wife, May-Britt, who both learned their craft at the Château Latour in Bordeaux. Together they composed a Bordeaux-style Cabernet Sauvignon that is dense and beautifully textured, with power and depth yet is elegant and dancing with layers of flavor.

To set their wine apart from the many lovely Cabernet Sauvignons on the market, Ali and Kambiz chose the name Xurus, which comes from their own rich culture and from Zoroastrian philosophy. The word *xurus* (pronounced "khoo-roos") means "rooster" in Persian. In Persian tradition, the crowing of the xurus signals the transition from the evil of darkness to the goodness of daylight and it also symbolizes hope and transformation, the dawn of a new day.

To capture this spirit, an icon composed of two roosters was developed and incorporated into an elaborately drawn border, signifying the close relationship and collaboration of the two proprietors, Ali and Kambiz. The labels were printed using a classic letterpress, a process hundreds of years old. Here the artwork is set into metal plates, and then the raised surface is inked and pressed into a sheet of paper. The resulting image comes out elegantly printed with an embossed feel. This is the process invented by Johannes Gutenberg in the mid-fifteenth century and was the industry standard well into the nineteenth century. As is evident in the Xurus label, this process produces an amazingly tactile result, giving the ornate design of the rooster incredible detail, texture and authenticity. The package design is as opulent as the wine itself.

Capp Heritage Vineyards

COMPANY   HERITAGE VINEYARDS OF NAPA, LLC, NAPA, CALIFORNIA
APPELLATION NAPA VALLEY, CALIFORNIA

"Vine planting is like the beginning of mining for precious metals," wrote Robert Louis Stevenson after visiting California's vineyards during the early 1880s.

Stevenson would have loved Capp Heritage Vineyards, for it has roots tracing back to both the Gold Rush and the first wine cultivation in Napa Valley. According to family records and lore, David Hudson and his future wife, Frances Griffith–Daniel Capps' great-great grandparents– came to California in 1845 on the first wagon train to cross the Sierra Nevada into California. David and Frances carried with them everything they needed to survive, including a rugged pioneer spirit.

And they needed it. In 1846, fearing for their lives, the Hudson family participated in the Bear Flag Revolt, which led to California's independence from Mexico. Two years later, the Hudsons were up in the Sierra Nevada Mountains panning for gold, and their efforts resulted in enough gold to purchase a plot of prime farmland in the heart of Napa Valley. David and his family also built the first cabins in what is now Calistoga and the first homes in what is now St. Helena. The Hudsons then made their mark in the history of California

wine by planting some of the very first vineyards that supplied grapes to the first commercial winery in Napa.

Today, four generations later, Daniel and Marguerite Capp reverently honor their family's tradition with a line of wines that pays tribute to the bounty of the Napa Valley and to the industry their ancestors helped launch over one hundred and sixty years ago.

For CF Napa, the key to the project would be to celebrate their family's exceptional history, but to do so in a thoroughly contemporary way. For inspiration, we poured through historic land deeds, documents and countless family stories. The resulting label features a timeless etching of a farmer working his field with a horse-drawn plow. The image is staged on a layered background of calligraphy derived from an old land deed from Daniel's great-great-grandfather, David Hudson. A custom monogram was developed as part of the icon, along with a hand-drawn wordmark that echoes the typography of the early history of the American West. Finally, a gold cigar-band-like graphic was printed on the capsule. The finished package for Capp Heritage is one of refined elegance.

VINT **2010** DATE

CAPP HERITAGE
— Vineyards —

NAPA VALLEY
CABERNET SAUVIGNON

OVER 160 YEARS

ESTD 1845

*Over a hundred and sixty years of family
heritage in the Napa Valley.*

1070 Green

COMPANY McGah Family Cellars, Alamo, California
APPELLATION Rutherford, Napa Valley, California

The McGah family vineyard is located on sixty-four acres of rich, gravelly loam in Rutherford, one of the most prized regions for growing top-quality Napa Valley fruit. With its warm days and cool nights, the McGahs' corner of the Rutherford Bench is ideal for growing Sauvignon Blanc. The name 1070 Green is a tribute to the family's longtime home address in San Francisco. The McGah home in the City by the Bay was often the gathering place for festive family get-togethers and holidays, so it was fitting that the address should take on a new life as a wine brand symbolizing the spirit of family and friends joining in celebration.

When the McGahs came to CF Napa, they wanted a clean, modern design that would reinforce the brand name and the crisp flavors of the Sauvignon Blanc and that would allow the package to "breathe." The resulting design is a modern mosaic of greens inspired from the brand name, which is represented both in words and numbers. When combined, these two expressions of the name allow the viewer to respond to the brand name verbally while still presenting the numeric address. The numbers and brand typography are debossed into the richly textured label to provide further definition. The various shades of green pay tribute to the name and also provide wonderful flavor cues for the bright, crisp Sauvignon Blanc inside.

Painted Rock

COMPANY PAINTED ROCK ESTATE WINERY, PENTICTON, BRITISH COLUMBIA, CANADA
APPELLATION OKANAGAN VALLEY, BRITISH COLUMBIA

John Skinner's day job was in investment banking, but his larger ambition in life was to create a world-class red wine in the Bordeaux tradition. In pursuit of that dream, John and his wife, Trish, purchased a jewel: a spectacular property overlooking the eastern shore of Skaha Lake in Penticton, British Columbia. This sixty-acre tract has a microclimate ideally suited to the production of premium wines.

On their property, on bluffs behind where the vineyards are today, John discovered some ancient pictographs painted on the rocks. John consulted the native First Nations band and learned that the pictographs were symbolic of a spirit walk, of a momentous "coming of age." As soon as he heard that, John realized he had found the perfect name for their new family estate: Painted Rock. In search of fitting imagery and feel, John came to CF Napa.

Several wineries in the Okanagan region were already using petroglyphs on their labels, and we felt this sort of imagery was not appropriate for higher-end wines. Instead, we chose the path of abstract minimalism, with two exquisite swirls suggesting rocks. The rocks were painted with a Japanese horse brush and printed on the label with a translucent pearl foil. To add dimension and texture, we added a rich sculptural emboss to the icon and overprinted it with two subtle inks to augment the effect.

The resulting label conveys an air of mystery, as well as a clean, modern classicism. Painted Rock has since become a star of the Okanagan region and a top-rated cult wine. John and Trish Skinner believe, of course, that all this was meant to be, that their destiny in Okanagan was magically written right on those rocks.

PAINTED ROCK

RED WINE | VIN ROUGE

Red Icon

ESTATE GROWN

OKANAGAN VALLEY

2007

ANATOMY

№1

GROWN & PRODUCED
—IN—
NAPA VALLEY

HIGH QUALITY & REFINED
CABERNET SAUVIGNON
—Bottled in the year of—
2006

· FEATURES ·

Dark features, long, inviting legs and a
medium body. Aromas of red and black fruits,
a hint of coffee: their combined silky kiss
leaves your taste buds lusting for more.

ALC. 13.9% BY VOL. 750ML

Anatomy

COMPANY HESPERIAN WINES, NAPA, CALIFORNIA

APPELLATION NAPA VALLEY, CALIFORNIA

Philippe Langner is a young winemaker from France who came to the US determined to innovate and also to celebrate the healthy, natural goodness of fine wine. He had the background for it. He studied agronomy at the University of California, Davis, and then trained in Bordeaux with two of the leading winemakers in the world, Jacques Boissenot and Michel Rolland. Philippe then moved to the Napa Valley and soon created his own company, Hesperian Wines.

Philippe has a playful turn of mind, and for his Anatomy brand he wanted a label that would stand out from the sea of other Napa Valley wines. He especially wanted to pay tribute to wine's cherished history as a restorative libation, a quality honored by doctors in many parts of the world and even in the Bible.

The resulting design takes its cues from the historic packaging of the elixirs that were offered as antidotes and cures for ailments during the early part of the twentieth century. The label's unexpected color and apothecary typography evoke the tonics and cure-alls that were so popular at that time. An interesting footnote: Philippe originally named the wine Antidote, but the Alcohol and Tobacco Tax and Trade Bureau (TTB), the government agency that oversees alcohol, rejected the name, arguing it was making health claims. We ultimately renamed the brand Anatomy, complete with tongue-in-cheek copy on the front label highlighting the wine's anatomy: dark features; long, inviting legs; and alluring body.

Gloria Ferrer Caves & Vineyards

LOCATION   SONOMA COUNTY, CALIFORNIA

In the early 1970s, Gloria Ferrer visited Sonoma County and immediately sensed its strong kinship with her native Spain. The rolling hills, the ideal weather, the sun shining brilliantly across the vineyards–all these touched her heart and fueled her imagination. Señora Ferrer wrote a letter to her husband, Jose Ferrer, the patriarch of the Ferrer family, who owned Freixenet, the eminent Spanish wine company whose roots trace back to the 1800s. She told Jose how much Sonoma reminded her of their native Catalonia, and she mused, "Wouldn't it be wonderful to spend time here, to plant vineyards and one day to make wine here in California?"

Her note struck a responsive chord with her husband, and in 1982 Gloria, Jose, and their eldest son, Pedro, returned to Sonoma County for a visit. Enchanted, they soon founded Gloria Ferrer Caves and Vineyards, devoted to crafting exquisite sparkling wines.

GLORIA FERRER SPARKLING WINES SONOMA, CALIFORNIA

Through the years, CF Napa has built a wonderful working relationship with Freixenet USA, and together we have stewarded many of its brands, including its line of sparkling wines. When Freixenet USA approached CF Napa to refresh its line of sparkling wines, the goal was to redesign the brand to be more premium while respectfully considering its key equity elements built over the previous thirty years. The label for the main tier of sparkling wines was inspired by the façade of the company's historic winery in Spain. Each of these labels has a debossed lineal pattern that provides texture to these classic yet singular labels. The capsules highlight the brand's nickname, Gloria, completing the warm personality of this popular Sonoma County brand.

PHOTO RIGHT: Gloria Ferrer Sparkling Wines

GLORIA FERRER CARNEROS CUVÉE SONOMA, CALIFORNIA

For its top offering, a "late disgorged" Carneros Cuvée, the Gloria
Ferrer team wanted to create an exceptional package; nothing
short of a trophy would do. The sparkling wine was to be laid
down to age for a full eight years before release, so the bottle and
label needed to exude a timeless elegance and grace that would
not feel dated when released eight years later. We started with a
single idea: Make each bottle a true collector's item. To that end,
we designed a sleek, distinctive, thoroughly modern shape for the
bottle, featuring an elegant curve in the glass. Then we designed
individualized, brass-riveted leather tags, to be attached to every
bottle of the exceptional cuvée. Each tag includes a space for the
winemakers to hand-write in the dates when that individual bottle
was disgorged and tiraged, making it a personalized keepsake for
the consumer. To finish it off, we designed a short, contemporary
capsule and neck wrap, creating a trophy-worthy look of elegance
and stunning modernity.

PHOTO RIGHT: *Gloria Ferrer Carneros Cuvée*

Est. 1975

2004

AMBER KNOLLS VINEYARD
CABERNET SAUVIGNON

The Seventy Five Wine Company

COMPANY   TUCK BECKSTOFFER WINES, ST. HELENA, CALIFORNIA
APPELLATION   LAKE COUNTY, CALIFORNIA

In 1975 a young Tuck Beckstoffer and his family moved to the Napa Valley. Almost right away Tuck fell in love with farming and the winemaking process. As a teen, he worked in the vineyards of Napa and Mendocino counties, and during college he spent his summers working alongside some of the most influential winemakers in California. In 1997 Tuck produced a small amount of Cabernet Sauvignon under the Tuck Beckstoffer label, and it quickly became one of the most acclaimed wines to come out of the Napa Valley. Seven years later, he created Tuck Beckstoffer Wines, now a portfolio of fine wines.

With The Seventy Five Wine Company, Tuck honors the year it all began. That was a turning point year for him and for many other pioneers as well. In 1975 a young techno whiz named Bill Gates founded a tiny start-up software company called Microsoft. That same year, the eloquent Russian dissident Andrei Sakharov was honored with the Nobel Peace Prize, creating one of the first significant cracks in the walls of the Soviet empire. And in 1975, a quirky TV show named *Saturday Night Live* made its debut and very quickly grew into an irreverent pillar of American popular culture. Tuck's wine pays tribute to all those things.

For the brand's packaging, Tuck wanted something clean, classy and fun, conveying that breakthrough spirit of 1975 and promising high quality at a reasonable price. Sometimes the solution for a great package can be the simplest of things; that was true here. The logo is built from the date 1975, with the *19* debossed into the paper and stamped in white pearl foil to create a subtle sheen. That places the *75* right on center stage. In addition, the hand-drawn *75* numerals are drawn with distinctly weighted "feet"–a conscious allusion to the 1970s fashion craze of bell-bottom pants, a theme we then built out with a fun lava lamp animation that we designed for the wine's website. Long live the 70s!

Atrea

COMPANY   SARACINA VINEYARDS, HOPLAND, CALIFORNIA
APPELLATION   MENDOCINO COUNTY, CALIFORNIA

When John Fetzer's family sold Fetzer Vineyards to the wine and spirits giant Brown-Forman in 1992, John planned on settling into a quiet life as a gentleman farmer in Mendocino County. For a decade, he replanted vineyards and put his expertise in organic grape-growing to work for a number of wineries in Napa and Sonoma counties. But then the itch returned, and John found himself missing the incomparable excitement of crafting his own fine wines.

In 2001 John and his wife, Patty Rock, set out to create a boutique winery that would showcase the varietals in which Mendocino County excels. The result was the Saracina Ranch and Vineyards, a six-hundred-acre biodiverse property extending across three separate ranches in Hopland, California. John and Patty have turned Saracina into a small-production, state-of-the-art California Certified Organic Farmers (CCOF) winery that features Mendocino varietals and also boasts

the first wine cave in Mendocino County. Atrea is a line that features lively Rhône-style red and white wines.

For Atrea's Old Soul Red and its classic white wine Atrea The Choir, CF Napa was asked to design a package that would appeal to the trendier, metropolitan segments of the East and West Coasts of the US. The resulting package is stark in its simplicity but rich in detail and finish. When developing brands for specific segments of the market, our inspiration often comes from other product categories that are part of our target consumers' larger lifestyle. Here, the inspiration for the label came from the elegant simplicity of high-end fragrances and health and beauty products. The solution stages a glossy black square within a white textural square, finished with a pearl white foil border, much like the silk finish on a fine tuxedo.

ATREA

OLD SOUL RED

Osoyoos Larose

LE GRAND VIN

2001

RED WINE · VIN ROUGE

MERLOT 66%

CABERNET SAUVIGNON 25%

CABERNET FRANC 9%

VQA OKANAGAN VALLEY

BRITISH COLUMBIA

Osoyoos Larose

COMPANY   Groupe Taillan of Bordeaux, France
and Constellation Brands, Canada, Inc., British Columbia, Canada

APPELLATION   Okanagan Valley, British Columbia

The Okanagan Valley is emerging as one of the wine world's most exciting new frontiers. Whereas much of British Columbia is cold and wet, this region, located in the interior of British Columbia, features a hot, dry, pocket desert called Osoyoos, an ideal environment for growing world-class grapes. The region is ringed by beautiful lakes and sage-covered mountains, which shield the area from the cold, wet weather systems that regularly roll in from the Pacific Ocean.

Okanagan is the home of Osoyoos Larose Le Grand Vin, a wine with an impressive pedigree of quality and character. The wine is a partnership of Groupe Taillan of Bordeaux, France, and Constellation Brands, Canada. They joined forces to create an exceptional Canadian wine using classic Bordeaux varietals, all grown on their arid, eighty-acre bench in the Okanagan Valley.

Constellation Brands asked CF Napa to create a brand that celebrated the wine's French heritage but also paid tribute to Okanagan's indigenous NK'MIP Indians (pronounced "in-Ka-meep") who have flourished in the Okanagan Valley for

thousands of years. To do that, we created a label that felt French but included border patterns found in the NK'MIP nation's indigenous artwork. In its simplicity and clean, structured layout, the resulting label is both classic and fresh. As a finishing touch, we created a rose icon, stamped in gold foil and embossed in a glossy white foil, helping it catch the light in a very evocative way.

Following the successful launch of Osoyoos Larose Le Grand Vin, Constellation Brands asked CF Napa to develop the line's second-growth wine. We named it Pétales d'Osoyoos, or Petals of Osoyoos, signifying the petals of a rose, and we designed a package that would fit easily within the new wine family but without losing its second-growth identity. For the new package, the rose icon of Le Grand Vin was redrawn into a long-stem rose, embossed in a subtle white foil. The brand name was then set off in an elegant script font to clearly differentiate it from Osoyoos Larose Le Grand Vin. Both wines have proved to be aesthetic and commercial triumphs.

PHOTO LEFT: *Osoyoos Larose*
PHOTO ABOVE: *Pétales d'Osoyoos*

Bench 1775

COMPANY   BENCH 1775, PENTICTON, BRITISH COLUMBIA, CANADA
APPELLATION   OKANAGAN VALLEY, BRITISH COLUMBIA

Jim Stewart came to wine via an usual route. A native of Vancouver, Jim trained as a lawyer, practiced business law for a time, and then found a whole new passion: computer animation. With Disney Studios as a primary client and Apple as his development partner, Jim founded his own animation software company in 1990. During his many business trips to California, Jim began visiting California wineries, and before long he got swept up in the romance and adventure of fine wine. First Jim became an investor in Paradise Ranch Wines Corp., an early pioneer in Canada's burgeoning wine export industry, then in 2011 he jumped in all the way, purchasing the struggling Soaring Eagle Estate Winery and its thirty-acre lake-front vineyard in British Columbia's scenic Okanagan Valley. In short order, Jim then turned the property into his own dream winery, Bench 1775.

Named for its address on Naramata Road, Bench 1775 is located on the renown Naramata Bench, a premier wine area in the Okanagan Valley. The name led us directly to the label design— a striking, artistic icon created by overlapping the individual numbers in 1775. Each numeral was custom drawn and debossed into the label to create a luxurious textured feel. We then created a distinctive wordmark by coupling the *h* in Bench with the *1* in 1775 for an elegant finishing touch. The result is a label of artistry and panache, mirroring Jim Stewart's own character and the spirit of his winery.

BENCH775

2011 CABERNET SAUVIGNON

VINTAGE VIN ROUGE | BC VQA OKANAGAN VALLEY

CHARDONNAY

2008
PINOT NOIR

MIGRATION

MIGRATION

ANDERSON VALLEY

Migration

COMPANY   DUCKHORN WINE COMPANY, ST. HELENA, CALIFORNIA

APPELLATION   RUSSIAN RIVER VALLEY, CALIFORNIA

The brand name, Migration, suggests the changing of seasons and birds winging their way across great sweeps of landscape. It is a perfect word for describing Duckhorn's line of Burgundian-style, cool-climate Pinot Noirs and Chardonnays, sourced from coastal vineyards in the Anderson and Russian River valleys and flyways.

In our view, the existing label for Migration felt too antiquated for wines of such exceptional vibrancy and finesse. Migration needed a new label that would better reflect the class and distinction that wine lovers would find inside the bottle. The existing painting on the label was a seaside landscape of ducks flying over a rocky coastline. We liked the basics of the imagery, but the classic nature of the artwork felt too dated and centered around the ocean, so we created a completely new illustration by rearranging the elements of the painting. The background was removed from the painting, and the ducks and sky were reworked into the classic *V* formation of migrating ducks. The new artwork far better expressed the feeling of movement and freedom of flight that are suggested by the name Migration.

To further enhance that feeling, we created a new wordmark with a custom-drawn letter *T* that has wing-like characteristics. We also placed a tiny arrow alongside the name to indicate the direction of movement. The imagery of the ducks became a unifying motif across many of the supporting elements for the brand, including the shipping cases where the ducks in flight stretch their way around two sides of the box.

Tapeña

LOCATION TIERRA DE CASTILLA, SPAIN

After working together for so many years, CF Napa and Freixenet are so attuned to one another that we can develop new ideas and new brands in almost seamless unison. And so it was with Tapeña. Jose Ferrer's team came to us wanting to launch a line of casual, hip Spanish wines for young consumers in the United States. But they also wanted to do something more: they wanted to introduce a whole new generation of US wine drinkers, the millennials, to the feel and spirit of Spain itself.

This was a stimulating challenge. To engage millennials, we knew we had to break away from traditional wine names, labels, and anything that suggested Old World. Our aim was to capture the essence of modern Spain in the new wine's name, label, and supporting marketing campaign.

We began by reviewing extensive consumer research and focus groups. We found that for millennials, Spain meant the warmth of the sun on your face, friendly, family-style meals and *chispa*, a word that translates to an intangible "spark of life." At the time when this brand was being created, tapas restaurants, with their distinctive Spanish appetizer-like small dishes, were springing up all over the United States, setting in motion a whole new food and bistro craze. That inspired an idea: fuse the word *tapas* with the Spanish word *peña*, a popular slang term for a group of pals or for a small, trendy club. The result was a cool new brand name: Tapeña. It had an exotic ring, but it was also memorable and easy to pronounce: "Tah-PAY-nyah."

PHOTO RIGHT: *Tapeña*

Tapeña
TEMPRANILLO
PRODUCT OF SPAIN
VINTAGE
2005
Tapeña
GARNACHA
PRODUCT OF SPAIN

Then we went further. Like many bistros in Europe, the tapas bars in Barcelona feature daily menu specials that are scrawled in chalk on small blackboards and then are hung on the wall or brought to your table. Those specials are often served communal style; everyone digs in with their own fork. Bingo! We crafted a playful fork, scrawled in chalk, and made it the signature image for the brand. Everyone loved that fork: it made for a fresh, original, free-flowing logo, and it was a perfect match for our engaging call-to-action tagline: "Grab a fork!"

We had a winner: the name and the branding clicked. After its launch in 2008, Freixenet shipped more than fifty thousand cases of Tapeña in the first 16 months, with placements in more than twenty-five key retail chains. Within a year, more than a quarter of a million people had visited the company's website, and by 2010 Tapeña ranked in the top-ten, per-volume Spanish table wines. Today, Spanish wines remain one of the hottest sectors of the market, and Tapeña is not only one of the fastest-growing Spanish brands in the United States; it is also enjoying growing popularity internationally. Those are results that translate easily in any language.

PHOTO LEFT: *Tapeña Bus Shelter Advertisement*
PHOTO RIGHT: *Tapeña Point of Sale Materials*

WINDMILL VALLEY

VINEYARDS

2012

CABERNET SAUVIGNON

Napa Valley

Windmill Valley Vineyards

COMPANY DAVIS ESTATES, CALISTOGA, CALIFORNIA
APPELLATION CALISTOGA, CALIFORNIA

It began with a blind date. Mike Davis was fixed up with Sandy Farquhar, and the two of them went for a walk along Huntington Beach, south of Los Angeles. Right away they clicked on several levels. Mike was a sales ace, and Sandy was a registered nurse with a definite entrepreneurial spirit. They married in 1982, and in 1989 they launched a new venture out of their garage— a computer hardware company called Applied Computer Solutions, or ACS.

ACS grew rapidly into a multifaceted IT solutions company, serving several major high-tech firms, and together Mike and Sandy produced sales figures of over one billion dollars. But as he and Sandy built their business and raised their two sons, Mike harbored a secret dream: to settle in the Napa Valley and make fine wine.

That dream has since become a reality. Mike and Sandy now have a home in Rutherford, in the central portion of the Napa Valley, and in 2011 they purchased the prestigious Saviez Vineyards, just south of the town of Calistoga. They are planning to make a broad variety of exclusive, small-production wines with a commitment to sustainable practices and support of their local community. As a symbol of this commitment to nature and sustainability, Mike and Sandy have erected a signature windmill on their property.

For this project, CF Napa began by exploring ways to render the estate's windmill as the icon. We drew a number of different renditions of the windmill, both abstract and photographic, and ultimately we settled on a bold graphic style that provides a sense of luxury. The windmill icon was drawn with a heroic stature in bold silhouette, and for the label, we embossed and stamped it in gold foil as a juxtaposition to the rich black background. The resulting label has an understated elegance that captures the historic nostalgia of the windmill on a contemporary label that is as timeless as the estate itself.

Black Sage Vineyard

COMPANY   CONSTELLATION BRANDS CANADA, INC., BRITISH COLUMBIA, CANADA
APPELLATION   OKANAGAN VALLEY, BRITISH COLUMBIA, CANADA

Black Sage Vineyard has a sumptuous home: a pocket desert in Canada's beautiful Okanagan Valley. Here, sunlight paints the rugged landscape with vibrant tones that dance across the valley's canyon walls, creating a bold, ever-changing tapestry of light that helps produce the region's unique winegrowing terrain. Black Sage has an unusual climate: hot and arid by day but cooled at night by breezes from nearby Lake Osoyoos. During the winter, the granite cliffs bordering the Black Sage Vineyard capture the heat of the day and protect the vines from frost and freezing. This sheltered locale, plus its sandy soil and excellent drainage, creates a muscular vineyard that produces truly exceptional wines.

Constellation Brands Canada asked CF Napa to create a new design for the brand's line of premium Black Sage wines for its larger Sumac Ridge brand. The new line would feature big, brawny red wines and would be named after the vineyard itself. Aimed primarily at male consumers, the Black Sage Vineyard packaging would need to communicate

the bold, luscious style of the wines and exude a masculine feel, yet remain refined enough to communicate the premium quality of the wines and to justify their higher target price.

Inspiration was drawn from both the rugged nature of the Black Sage Vineyard's terroir and climate as well as from many of today's bourbon and whiskey packages. These, after all, are some of the ultimate examples of packaging created to appeal to men. The result exudes a rugged masculinity. On the label, we stamped a large, weathered wordmark, overlaid by a short evocation of the Black Sage story. The cream color of the background evokes the rich loam of the vineyard, while the deep red and black highlights add a definite swagger. The varietals are signaled confidently in black boxes to create a strong, quick read, and the massive vintage date is stamped right into the label, bleeding off the edge, creating a package that balances luxury with brash masculinity—the true essence of the brand.

N49° 06.890' | W119° 32.485'

BLACK
SAGE
VINEYARD

THE NORTHERN MOST POINT OF THE SONORA
DESERT IS CANADA'S BEAUTIFUL OKANAGAN
VALLEY, HOME TO BLACK SAGE VINEYARD.

RED WINE | VIN ROUGE

BC VQA OKANAGAN VALLEY

CABERNET SAUVIGNON

2010

Riverbench

COMPANY   RIVERBENCH VINEYARD & WINERY, SANTA MARIA, CALIFORNIA
APPELLATION   SANTA MARIA VALLEY, CALIFORNIA

Riverbench has deep roots in Santa Barbara County. The vineyard is located on a spectacular bench beside the Sisquoc River in the heart of the lovely Santa Maria Valley, one of California's most exciting winegrowing regions. The region boasts rich alluvial soils and microclimates that are ideal for growing Chardonnay, Pinot Noir and other noble varietals. For a winemaker, this is pretty close to heaven.

The Riverbench vineyard was originally planted in 1973, with the aim of growing top-quality Chardonnay and Pinot Noir grapes to be sold to various wineries in the region. For three decades, the owners of Riverbench did just that. In 2004, though, Riverbench was sold to a group of local families who had a much larger ambition: to create their own line of premium wines. And thus the Riverbench Vineyard & Winery was born.

The new owners of Riverbench came to CF Napa with a complicated challenge. Their original packaging had been crafted by a local designer, and consumers were not enthusiastic. Worse, their product line included a wide variety of looks for their various wines and was expensive to produce, especially for wines of very small production.

We began by working with Riverbench to simplify its product line into just two tiers, allowing it to significantly reduce its packaging logistics and costs. Next we redesigned its brand wordmark by spelling out Riverbench with an elegant combination of the second *R* in *River* and the *B* in *Bench*. This solution links the two initials so they stand happily together as a distinctive monogram. To highlight the winery's riverside location on the Santa Maria Bench, we developed a linocut print with a river running through it. We then over-stamped it with textured gold foil flecks, giving it the distinctive feel of an elegant jewel.

Educated Guess

COMPANY   ROOTS RUN DEEP WINERY, ST. HELENA, CALIFORNIA
APPELLATION   NAPA VALLEY, CALIFORNIA

Growing grapes and making superlative wines are not exact sciences. To the contrary, both emerge from long years of experience, intuition and the myriad choices made almost every day in the vineyards and wine cellars. Plain old good luck often plays a role too. With so many variables, it is no wonder that in wine circles you hear endless debates about what is more important: the hand of the winemaker or the hand of Mother Nature. Winemaker Mark Albrecht honors these inherent uncertainties with the name Educated Guess, the first release and the flagship brand of his young Napa Valley winery, Roots Run Deep. The name also contains a subtle appeal to today's wine consumer, who too often enters a wine shop or a supermarket and is confronted with a bewildering array of hundreds of bottles and labels. Faced with so many choices, how is a consumer supposed to make a sound buying decision? Well, just make "an educated guess."

For CF Napa, the challenge here was complex: to convey the brand's quirky spirit on the label yet remain sophisticated enough for the wine's price point. The answer is one of the more distinctive labels in American wine. The rich black label becomes the blackboard for the handwritten formulas that occur naturally in the winemaking process or are induced by the skilled winemaker. The formulas are scrawled across the label as if some fevered Einstein of winemaking were exploring the creative and scientific limits of what can be created. Although the formulas we put on the label are real, you do not need to be a chemistry major to get the message: making superlative wine is both a science and an exalted art form, as just a few sips of Educated Guess will make deliciously clear.

Educated
Guess

x (NAPA VALLEY + 2005)

CABERNET SAUVIGNON

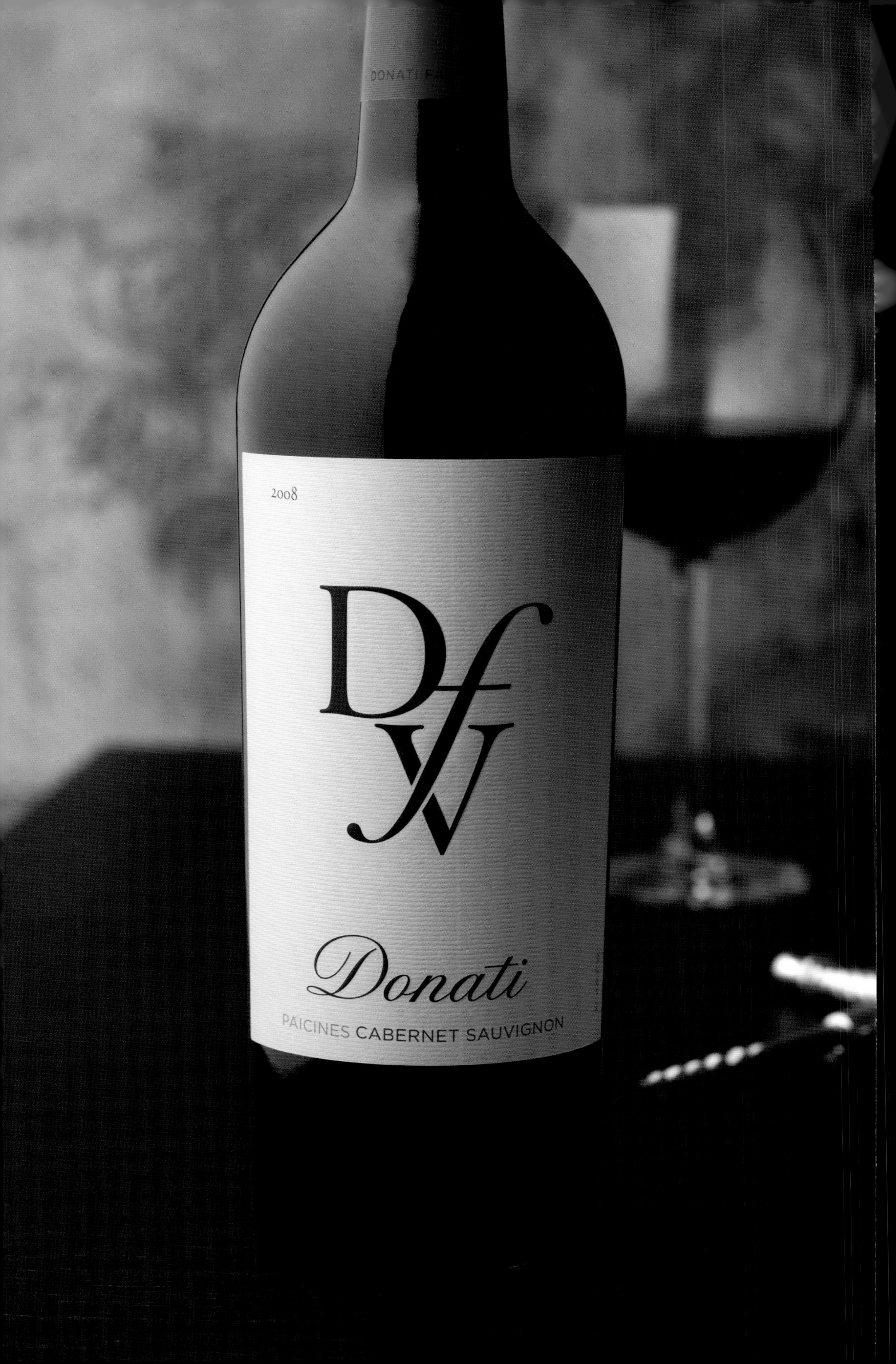
DONATI FA
2008
DV
Donati
PAICINES CABERNET SAUVIGNON

DFV

COMPANY   DONATI FAMILY VINEYARD, TEMPLETON, CALIFORNIA
APPELLATION CALIFORNIA CENTRAL COAST, CALIFORNIA

The town of Paicines is a tiny dot on the map of California, located right in the center of the state, a bit inland from the Pacific Coast. Vineyards have existed in the region since the era of the Spanish missionaries, but as late as forty years ago the vineyards there were devoted almost exclusively to mass-production wines. No longer. Early on, Ron Donati saw the area's potential and bought a large property with the hope that his sons, Brad, Mark and Matt, would one day grow premium grapes there. That dream has now been realized: in Paicines the Donatis are now producing an exceptional line of wines under the label DFV, for Donati Family Vineyard.

The Donatis came to CF Napa to redesign their logo and their main line of DFV wines. At the time, the Donatis had an existing seal on their packaging, and they felt it had some equity. But we saw a strong opportunity to move their brand to a more contemporary expression of their pioneering story. The result is a package that is at once contemporary and classically timeless. The DFV initials were crafted to become a modern monogram for their winery. We embossed and enhanced the monogram by adding a high-build matte silk screen. A new script was drawn for their Donati wordmark, communicating a high level of European-style sensibility and also providing readability across all of the Donatis' corporate materials and wearables. The label's background was then embossed with a custom-laid finish, giving the label a rich textural feel and putting a high shine on their iconic new label.

Canopy Management

When Terry Wheatley turned fifty, she made a momentous decision. She had learned the wine business—and marketing—from the ground up, working for two of the biggest powerhouses in the California wine industry: Gallo and Sutter Home. Over the years, Terry had seen and understood the transformation of consumer sensibilities, and she had seen the rising importance of female consumers. One day Terry had a revelation: she would go out on her own and put her nontraditional marketing ideas into practice.

She created Canopy Management, a Napa-based boutique wine company that creates fresh, fun wine brands aimed directly at female consumers—and all priced under fifteen dollars a bottle. Terry's gamble has paid off: Canopy's portfolio of wines is impressive, and it has built a strong following for its wines by developing relationships with key retailers and by the very clever use of digital media and social networking. For instance, its website, winesisterhood.com, promotes its brands to consumers and encourages them to join "The Wine Sisterhood." Also featuring wine-inspired recipes, travel ideas and entertaining tips, the website has become a popular venue for consumers to discuss wine and much more. To further build its following, The Wine Sisterhood hosts annual get-togethers—an ideal way to promote its brands and help women learn more about wines and winemaking.

COWGIRL SISTERHOOD CALIFORNIA

Over the years, Terry Wheatley has come to CF Napa with hundreds of unusual brand concepts, some serious, some fun, and a few just plain crazy. A case in point: her concept for a new brand called the Cowgirl Sisterhood, a brand that would be built around a sweet red and a sweet white wine. Our creative brief was to craft a look and feel that would appeal to the "cowgirl" consumer. "Think 'big as Texas'," Terry told us, "and all that comes with it." The packaging we envisioned together would symbolize cow-poke country, while retaining a quintessentially feminine attitude.

We drew our primary inspiration from the playful imagery found on the saloon posters of the Old West and then "purdied" it up a bit. For the red wine, we used a reddish purple label with the name stamped in flashy gold foil, and for the white wine, we used a gold label stamped with the name scrawled in bright lipstick red. Spread above the name are the wings of a classic emblem, the eagle, and under it is an eclectic stack of typography. The message on each bottle will make you smile: "The most down home, lip smackin' darn tootin' purdiest wine you'll ever taste." The final touch was to emboss and overprint the labels with a soft-touch tactile varnish, giving the finish of the labels the rich, luxurious feel of well-worn leather.

MONOGAMY LAKE, MENDOCINO AND SONOMA COUNTIES, CALIFORNIA

Monogamy was built on the knowledge that many wine consumers are loyal to their favorite varietals–and that variety is not necessarily the spice of life. Terry's guiding idea here was to give female drinkers permission to be loyal and faithful to their favorite wine. In other words, an old-fashioned virtue in marriage could also be a virtue with regard to wine.

To make that concept work, we felt the front label should be kept simple and honest. Our approach features a bright wedding-dress-white paper embossed with a rich texture and finished with a pearl white foil border. We put a subtle twist on the Monogamy wordmark by replacing the letter O at the center with a red heart icon. Underneath the wordmark reads the message: "Truly, Madly, Deeply." Each of the back labels professes love for the varietal of choice. In the case of the Cabernet Sauvignon, the back label carries an endorsement of monogamy:

"You know you've experimented. It's a way to discover what you like. And what you don't. What makes you happy. What satisfies your soul. It's how you know when you've found the one. The one that makes you say, 'Sorry, I'm with Cabernet.' When you've met the love of your life, is there really any reason to keep looking?"

This playful brand concept has proved to be a winner for Terry; these wines have become known as ideal for engagements, weddings, anniversaries and for those times when you just need to get back into the good graces of the one you love.

monogamy

TRULY MADLY DEEPLY

NORTH COAST
CABERNET SAUVIGNON

2006

CHATEAU
FONPLEGADE

GRAND VIN DE BORDEAUX

Grand Cru Classé

SAINT-EMILION GRAND CRU

2010

S & D Adams, Propriétaires
PRODUIT DE FRANCE

Château Fonplégade

COMPANY CHÂTEAU FONPLÉGADE, SAINT-ÉMILION, FRANCE
APPELLATION SAINT-ÉMILION, FRANCE

Château Fonplégade has a distinguished history in France and beyond. Located just outside the enchanting village of Saint-Émilion, the chateau is one of Bordeaux's oldest wine properties. In 1853 the chateau was sold to the Duke of Morny, who was the half brother of Napoleon III. The chateau changed hands several times until 2004, when it was purchased by two Americans, Denise and Stephen Adams.

Today, the chateau's elegant façade and Roman pathways pay homage to its glorious roots, as does a lovely Roman fountain on the property, the inspiration for the name of the chateau: Fonplégade, literally meaning "Fountain of Plenty." Denise and Stephen Adams have meticulously renovated the chateau and its vineyards, and they have put into place an ambitious biodynamics program, with the guidance of the esteemed wine consultant Michel Rolland. The soil they work is rich in limestone and clay and nourished in drier years by deep underground springs.

The Adams came to CF Napa with an exciting challenge: to refresh their packaging for Château Fonplégade Grand Cru Classé and their second-growth Fleur de Fonplégade, as well as to design the packaging for their new wine, Fleur de Fonplégade Rosé. The task was daunting, as the equity elements of the brand were hundreds of years old and well established in Saint-Émilion. To start, the wordmark was refreshed and made more readable, without disturbing its traditional cachet. We then commissioned new engravings that would accurately depict the refurbished state of the chateau and its landscaping, bringing the iconography fully up to date.

The fountain, with its storied Roman past at the heart of Château Fonplégade, makes for a perfect icon for the second-growth. This label features an elegant combination of typography with the new engravings as the centerpiece of the labels. The engravings are printed in the same ageless olive green color that had been used for years on their labels. For their new Rosé, we created a signature rose, embossed and stamped in a white foil on bright white paper, providing a subtle highlight on the label and letting the beauty of the wonderfully pink wine come shining through.

PHOTO LEFT: *Château Fonplégade Grand Cru Classé*
PHOTO ABOVE LEFT: *Fleur de Fonplégade Second-Growth*
PHOTO ABOVE RIGHT: *Fleur de Fonplégade Rosé*

Luna Nuda

COMPANY
APPELLATION

LUNA NUDA WINES, ATLANTA, GEORGIA
ALTO ADIGE, ITALY

In Italian, Luna Nuda means "naked moon," and Italian winemakers use the phrase to refer to a clear night sky with a bright full moon shimmering across their vineyards. Bathed in such an auspicious light, what winemaker could fail to be stirred? And what vineyard could fail to bring forth the most heavenly fruit? That was the inspiration for Luna Nuda Wines.

Luna Nuda's light, fruity Pinot Grigio grapes are sourced from a fourth-generation vineyard in northern Italy's Alto Adige region, one of the world's best for producing Pinot Grigio. The folks at Luna Nuda knew the quality of their wines was exceptional, but when they launched their new brand in the southeastern US, the initial sales were very disappointing. When they actually tasted the wine, US consumers loved this bright, elegant wine, but the packaging was unappealing, and it hampered sales.

Luna Nuda's original label was a tired cliché: a gondolier navigating the canals of Venice by night. That image gave absolutely no hint of the quality of the wine inside the bottle. If the folks at Luna Nuda were ever going to get traction for their brand, they knew they had to make some dramatic changes. That is why they came to us.

We loved the name, and we kept the shimmering night sky as our imagery, but the entire package would require a revamp. Our aim was to make the brand much more premium in appearance and to have it pop off of retailers' shelves. The new logo mark features a shining moon fashioned from tiny, hand-drawn stars. Those stars are stamped in gold foil and overprinted with three different inks, giving them rich depths of gold patina. We then embossed them in such a way that the stars literally twinkle as light reflects off the bottle. As a final touch, on the capsule we reproduced the midnight blue of that romantic Italian night sky. Who could possibly resist?

ITALIA

LUNA NUDA

ITALIA

2010

PINOT GRIGIO

Vigneti delle Dolomiti

INDICAZIONE GEOGRAFICA TIPICA

Cycles Gladiator

COMPANY   Hahn Family Wines, Napa, California

APPELLATION   Central Coast, California

The spirit of California's Central Coast is fresh and wild. Its rugged, untamed Pacific coastline, its sprawling pine forests and its breathtaking views—these have long attracted painters, photographers, writers and adventurers like John Steinbeck and Henry Miller. And today the Central Coast remains a sensory feast, a place to dream, a place to live, a place to breathe and create, unencumbered and free.

The Hahn family, with its deep roots in Monterey County, set out to capture that spirit in a special line of wines, each celebrating the area's artistic and Bohemian roots. In the family's eyes, the brand packaging would need to be characteristically Californian but with a definite European flair. For inspiration, we looked at many paintings and drawings before zeroing in on the classic French posters that adorned Paris bistros back in the 1890s. And then we found it: a poster trumpeting a new brand of bicycles, Cycles Gladiator.

The original poster was created by G. Massias in 1895, and its name and imagery seemed a perfect fit for Nicky Hahn's line of fresh, exciting wines.

We reworked the poster and its typography into a label with bold colors, swirling movement and an exhilarating feeling. The label features a nude woman with a swirling mane of red hair, riding a winged bike through a midnight sky—a vision of unbridled sensuality and spirit, a beautiful and arresting image of personal and artistic freedom.

The imagery worked wonderfully for the brand. Consumers loved it; bottles flew off the shelves; and the Cycles Gladiator label was so successful that we have since extended the brand to a whole line of wines featuring European poster art centered on bicycles and serving as a natural hook for marketing campaigns targeting avid bicycle riders. The success of Cycles Gladiator also came with a delicious whiff of controversy: the brand was actually banned in Alabama due to the sensuous nudity on the label. Hahn responded with a tongue and cheek wine brand appropriately named Banned in Bama Cuvée.

PHOTO LEFT: *Cycles Gladiator*
PHOTO ABOVE LEFT: *Cycles Clement*
PHOTO ABOVE RIGHT: *Cycles Falcon*

Voveti

COMPANY Freixenet, Spain and Eugenio Collavini, Italy

APPELLATION Veneto D.O.C., Italy

As every traveler quickly discovers, Italy is effervescent. Its people are fun, friendly, charming and informal. The same can be said for Prosecco, the vivacious, fruit-rich Italian sparkling wine that is proving increasingly popular across the US. In this exciting and expanding terrain, the Spanish sparkling wine powerhouse Freixenet decided to introduce its own brand of Italian Prosecco. To do this, Freixenet joined hands with the Collavini family, the acclaimed master craftsmen of Italian sparkling wines. From their base in the region of Corno di Rosazzo, in the northeast corner of Italy, the Collavinis for generations have crafted sparkling wines that are praised for their exceptional spirit and finesse.

To help them develop this new brand, Freixenet USA, a longtime client, came to CF Napa. Our mission: to craft a name for the new Prosecco and also design the brand's identity, packaging and marketing materials. We started the process by reviewing the competition among Proseccos in the US market and abroad, and right away we saw a big opportunity. Most of the Prosecco brands already on the shelf were staid and conservative. We believed that a fresh, modern offering could really stand up and sing, and do so with enormous promise. That led to the name Voveti. The word comes from the Latin root *voveo*, a verb meaning to "vow" or "promise," and we saw the name as a perfect salute to the promise of this new partnership and to the exciting quality of the new wine itself.

For the packaging, we took our inspiration directly from modern Italian fashion and fragrance. The bottle has a sleek feminine quality, and the label is a glossy, almost wet-looking black. Like chic Italian leather goods, it has a high-fashion feel with a custom-pebbled texture. Against that black composition, we present the Voveti wordmark with an O that stands out elegantly in a bright peach-orange color, quietly signaling the wonderful melon and ripe peach flavors of the wine. That O is composed of two interlocking rings, symbolizing the joint two families' "vow" and finishing the package with graceful Italian flair.

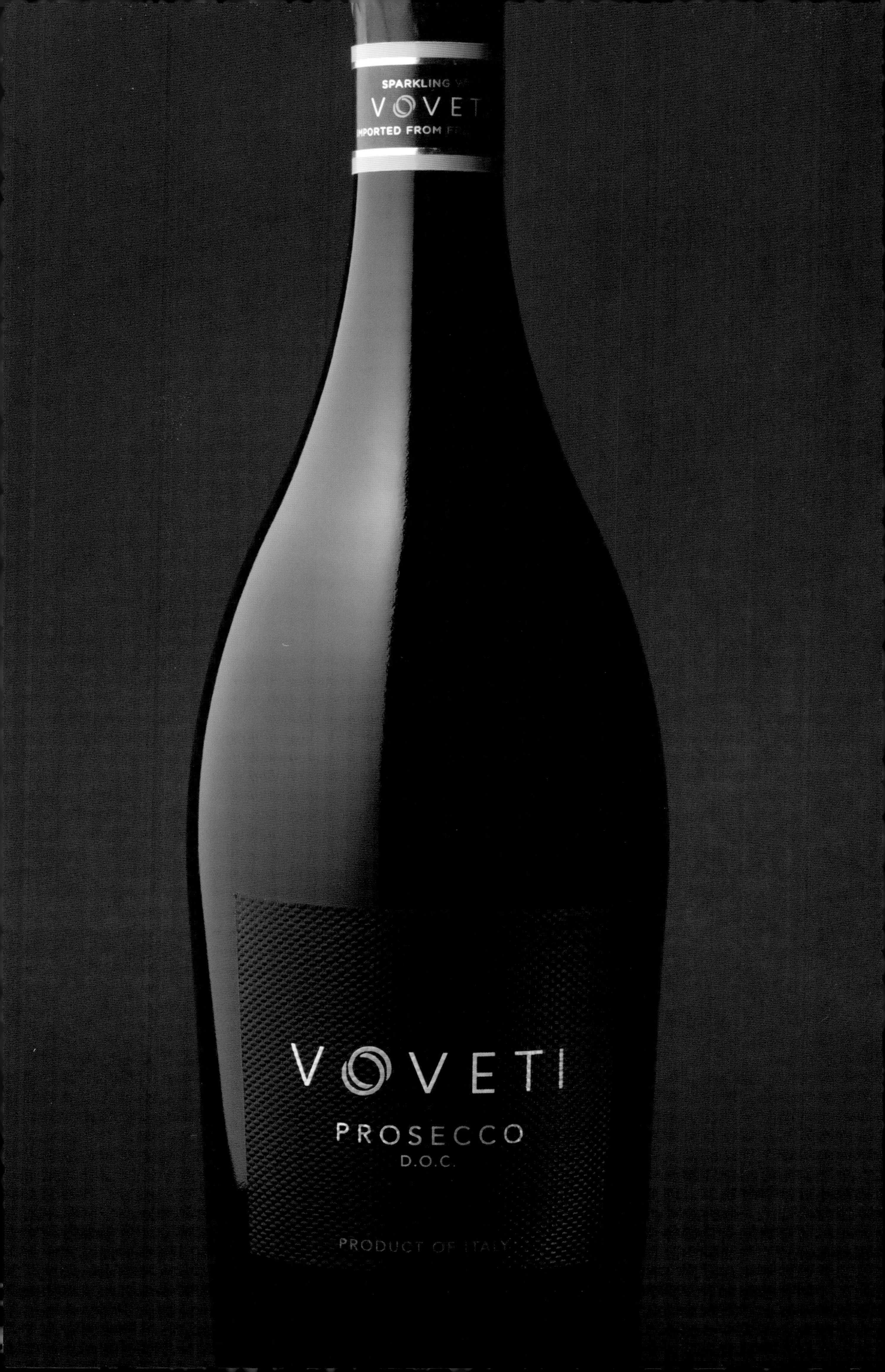
SPARKLING
VOVETI
PROSECCO
D.O.C.
PRODUCT OF ITALY

Dancing Coyote

COMPANY   DANCING COYOTE WINES, ACAMPO, CALIFORNIA

APPELLATION   CLARKSBURG, CALIFORNIA

The McCormack family has been farming in California's verdant Sacramento River Delta for five generations, and coyotes play a starring role in their family lore. Legend has it that each year at the beginning of the growing season, a band of coyotes from the nearby foothills would sneak into the family vineyards in Clarksburg and, for no good reason, start chomping on their irrigation lines with crazed abandon. This was treachery, pure and simple, and after feasting, the coyotes would dance wildly around, howling at the moon in joyous celebration.

The McCormacks' line of wines includes a rich variety of affordable and distinctive wines, including Albariño, Grüner Veltliner and Verdelho. But soon they ran into a problem. Yes, the brand name was colorful, and the wines were bold and authentic, but the brand's wines just did not sell as well as expected. The feedback from retailers was the packaging was not commensurate with the quality of their wines and even at times had become a barrier to sale.

When the McCormacks came to CF Napa, we quickly pinpointed the problem. The labels and packaging were rendered with a gloomy color palette, and the graphics were reminiscent of the old Looney Toons cartoon graphics. Also, their white wines were bottled in a dark, unappealing colored glass–a poor way to showcase the bright, refreshing characteristics of the white wine inside. We made several changes. The bottles for the white wines were changed to clear flint, far better for housing crisp, refreshing varietals like their Albariño. The labels were redesigned, using a bright, cream-colored paper, a rich embossed texture and a nontraditional type stack, giving the label a more artistic and worldly feel. We redrew the dancing coyote icon–cut out as a linocut– to give it a more authentic, textural, boutique sensibility. The guiding idea was to refresh the brand to be more in line with the contemporary consumer tastes for such distinguished varietals. Our efforts paid off: with these fundamental design changes, those zany coyotes began dancing happily off retailers' shelves.

Crew Wine Company

Lane Giguiere and her husband, John, have had an incredible journey. They met in high school in California's Yolo County, the fertile agricultural region northwest of Sacramento, and they married soon thereafter. In 1973 John and Lane and John's older brother, Karl, decided to return to the Giguiere's twenty-seven-hundred-acre farm in the Dunnigan Hills, where the brothers grew up. The trio envisioned an idyllic life working the land, raising sheep and growing wheat. By then, though, many family farms nearby were dying a slow death, but something new was on the rise: wine.

Not one of their neighbors was growing grapes, but the Giguieres made a leap of faith and planted ten acres of Sauvignon Blanc and Chenin Blanc. In 1984 they launched R.H. Phillips, producing four thousand cases of wine–and selling every drop. And that was just the beginning. The following year they sold forty thousand cases of estate-bottled, premium and super premium wines, and from there they just kept on growing. In 2000 the Giguieres sold the company to the Canadian giant Vincor International. John and Lane used the proceeds to launch a new venture, the Crew Wine Company, intent on producing premium wines. It was then that John came to CF Napa; he and Lane wanted help launching two wine brands: Matchbook and Sawbuck.

MATCHBOOK DUNNIGAN HILLS, CALIFORNIA

John Giguiere was a high-spirited child. As a farm kid growing up in the late 1950s and early 1960s, he became known as a bit of a pyromaniac, setting all sorts of things on fire on his father's wheat farm. His brother, Karl, was no angel either. At one stage, fearing total ruin of his house and farm, their father took the boys to the city jail for an hour's stay to scare them out of their wits and to extinguish their fascination with fire. Undaunted, though, the boys then turned their attention to making and launching homemade rockets, which

often blew up, resulting in random fires on the farm and more exasperated calls to the local fire department. Fifty years later, those boyhood episodes led the Giguieres to launch a line of wines called Matchbook. For the design and packaging, we naturally needed to invoke a little pyromania, so we burned the edges of paper until we had the desired scorched effect for the label. Juxtaposed with modern typography and a blind-embossed flame icon, the label pays tribute to John and Karl's misspent youth.

SAWBUCK DUNNIGAN HILLS, CALIFORNIA

The backcountry hills and towns of Mendocino and Yolo counties
still have a touch of the Old West about them, and that provided
the perfect backdrop to the story of Sawbuck. The very first ten-
dollar bills in the United States were minted in the late 1800s,
bearing the Roman numeral X. In the eyes of many, that numeral
resembled the working man's wooden sawhorse, and thus was
born the nickname *sawbuck*.

In creating the packaging for this new wine, we researched the
original sawbuck bills and their varying designs over the years,
and we studied the currency's color palette, design style and
typography. Inspired, we fashioned the Sawbuck wordmark so
that it felt like an old engraving, complete with historic type and
a border system that looks like a security pattern, crafted by
repeating the brand name over and over. In our version, we
included a seal with a Roman numeral X–mimicking the Federal
Reserve Bank seal–and we added the winemaker and brand
owner's names in hand-drawn calligraphy, replacing the Secretary
of the Treasury's signature. We also included a serial number,
listing the number of bottles in each vintage's release. The result
is an engaging, respectful bow to a distinctive piece of US history.

ESTATE GROWN
CABERNET SAUVIGNON
NAPA VALLEY

2007

DAVIANA

WINEMAKER:

Daviana

COMPANY DAVIANA WINERY, NAPA, CALIFORNIA
APPELLATION COOMBSVILLE, NAPA VALLEY, CALIFORNIA

New Jersey native Tim Darrin has lived his life like the proverbial rolling stone. In college he studied art history, a subject that led him to travel the world, examining art and culture and furthering his studies in Switzerland. In the late 1970s, Tim "landed" in the Napa Valley–more times than you can count. You see, he and a couple friends created Adventures Aloft, the valley's first hot air balloon company, a business that kept Tim landing in Napa over and over–often near some of the finest vineyards in the world. Finally, Tim and his wife, Debbie, decided it was time to land in the middle of another vineyard–their own.

That decision led to the Daviana Winery, the Darrins' own winery in the newly recognized Coombsville appellation just east of the town of Napa. Theirs is a small, twenty-four-acre family estate producing high-quality Cabernet Sauvignon and Cabernache. In the early years, Tim and Debbie sold their grapes to premium wineries, but in 2005

they decided to launch their own wines under the label Daviana, a name derived from joining *David* and *Anna*, the middle names of their two children.

For CF Napa, the challenge was to capture the intimate family passion that drives Tim and Debbie, but to do so in a way that also conveyed the wine's classic, high-end Napa Valley style. They wanted something that would be understated yet high fashion at the same time. The solution centers around creating a distinctive brand icon: a hand-drawn *D* inspired by the Tuscan sensibilities of their estate and their wines. The label uses an asymmetric layout, with elegant scale and lots of luxurious white space. The finish is Tim's own signature, done in gold foil, making clear that this rolling stone now has roots deep in the golden Napa Valley soil.

Signorello Vineyards

COMPANY SIGNORELLO ESTATE, NAPA, CALIFORNIA
APPELLATION NAPA VALLEY, CALIFORNIA

One of the loveliest properties on the Napa Valley's Silverado Trail is Signorello Estate, a one-hundred-acre estate located between the towns of Napa and Yountville. Ray Signorello Sr. purchased the property in the mid-1970s with the aim of growing grapes and selling them to Napa Valley wineries. By 1985, though, Ray's vineyard was producing superb grapes, so he decided to shift to making wines under his own label. From then on, Ray and his son, Ray Jr., poured their hearts into crafting limited-production wines primarily from their estate vineyard in Napa Valley. Their winemaking philosophy combines European techniques and sensibilities with the opulent fruit of the Napa Valley. With his dad's death in 1998, Ray Jr. carries on the tradition of making world-class Napa Valley wine.

Seeking creative ways to continue to build its brand, Ray came to CF Napa. He wanted to refresh the packaging to better reflect the luxurious quality of the wines without losing core equity elements of the brand. In addition, he recognized a very functional need to more effectively differentiate between Signorello Estate's tiers of wines.

Our solution streamlined Signorello Estate's vineyard-designated wines into a more cohesive tier, while leaving its most exclusive wines, Hope's Cuvée and Padrone, as the star-studded iconic wines. We also completely redeveloped Signorello's logo. Still featuring Bacchus, the god of wine, the new logo is a more distinctive and dynamic rendition of Bacchus and has been given a stately, three-dimensional look through the use of embossed gold foil stamping that is then overprinted with a rich bronze patina.

SIGNORELLO

VINEYARDS

Napa Valley

CABERNET SAUVIGNON

2005

SIGNORELLO

VINEYARDS

Napa Valley
VIEILLES VIGNES
CHARDONNAY
2006

Estate Grown and Bottled

Estate Grown and Bottled
UNFILTERED

Bex

COMPANY PURPLE WINE COMPANY, GRATON, CALIFORNIA
APPELLATION MOSEL, GERMANY

Whether in New York, London, Paris or Berlin, many of today's wine drinkers are young, urban and wired into the world at large through the latest technology. With that in mind, the makers of BEX, a fresh, modern German Riesling, wanted to create a label and brand that would break away from stodgy European conventions and generate buzz among this new breed of young cosmopolitan wine drinkers.

For inspiration, CF Napa turned to Bauhaus design and the meld of precision engineering and high design of Germany's renowned auto brands. The result is a clean, innovative label featuring a metallic paper printed green to evoke the crisp apple accents of the Riesling inside the bottle. The label was embossed with a pleasing ribbed texture, giving the package a modern, sophisticated feeling. The large white brand name and clean design, more reminiscent of packaging for today's spirits brands than for wine, immediately set it apart from other wines and make it stand out on the back bar of hip bistros. The bold, contemporary typography and exactness of the BEX design are a tribute to its German heritage.

La Follette

COMPANY   LA FOLLETTE WINES, HEALDSBURG, CALIFORNIA

APPELLATION   SONOMA COAST, CALIFORNIA

Greg La Follette's first love was not wine; it was playing the bagpipes! But once he realized that the bagpipes provided no way to make a living, Greg set out to learn winemaking from the ground up. He earned a B.A. in plant biology and chemistry from California State University, Northridge, and then a master's degree in food science and technology at the University of California, Davis. There, Greg developed a special passion: understanding the texture of wine and the scientific components of the way wine feels in the mouth.

With that unusual passion and an accompanying love of Pinot Noir, Greg set off on a serious apprenticeship, working with the famed winemaker André Tchelistcheff at Beaulieu Vineyards and then at top wineries in Australia, Sonoma County and the Napa Valley. In 2009 Greg joined forces with Pete and Terri Kight, the owners of Quivira Vineyards & Winery in Dry Creek Valley. Together they created La Follette Wines with a clearly defined aim: to create lovely, cool-climate, small-lot premium appellated Pinot Noirs and Chardonnays.

When the La Follette team approached CF Napa, they wanted to build a brand based on Greg's expertise regarding texture and his idiosyncratic approach to winemaking. Greg is a true original. Part scientist, part "grape whisperer," Greg is known to talk to his vines, almost like a soothsayer, gently coaxing them along. He also listens to his wines during the fermentation process to determine how this key step is progressing.

For the brand design, we drew our inspiration from Greg's unusual blend of science and art. Our design team found an ancient text on winemaking that included a wonderful old engraving of a vigneron working on the trellising for his grapes. We reworked the engraving, removing the trellising tool and replacing it so the man was instead holding a "magic wand," like Greg, working miracles in the vineyard. We sourced notes from that same ancient text and added them to the illustration and the capsule to inject an element of science and history. The result is a package that feels classic yet contemporary, subtly capturing Greg's unusual guiding spirit.

LA FOLLETTE

vi. 2008

PINOT NOIR
Sonoma Coast

Fig. 1.   E,E, *Lignes de fil de fer galvanisé Nº 12.*
F,F, *Gros échalas bitumés de 9 à 10 cent. de tour (3 à 4 po) servant à soutenir les lignes de fer et placés à la distance de huit mètres l'un de l'autre.*
G,G, *Raidisseurs.*

LA FOLLETTE

TERRA VALENTINE

Estate Grown
CABERNET SAUVIGNON

NAPA VALLEY
SPRING MOUNTAIN DISTRICT

2007

Terra Valentine

COMPANY TERRA VALENTINE, NAPA, CALIFORNIA
APPELLATION SPRING MOUNTAIN DISTRICT, NAPA VALLEY, CALIFORNIA

Angus Wurtele is a cheerful mix of practical businessman and unabashed romantic. Angus grew up in Minnesota of Scottish-German and Quaker ancestry, and he first fell in love with the Napa Valley when he was earning his MBA at Stanford Business School. Back then, when he told his wife, Margaret, that one day they should retire to the Napa Valley, she just laughed at him: "You have a lot of crazy ideas. It will pass."

Evidently, the idea did not pass, and in 1995 the couple found their dream retirement spot—a lovely thirty-five acre property on Spring Mountain in Napa Valley, which they named Wurtele Vineyard. A few years later in 1999, the Wurteles bought a second winery property on Spring Mountain. It was here they founded Terra Valentine, after Angus's dad, Valentine, and planted twenty-five acres of vineyards.

In 2009 Terra Valentine came to CF Napa to modernize its packaging to make it more commensurate with the rising quality of its wines. The historic icon of St. Valentine was redrawn, his personage forming the shape of a heart. The icon, previously a colorful symbol, was changed to a more serious rich gold foil embossed and over-printed with a rich bronze patina. The labels for each tier of the wines were then redesigned to more clearly differentiate the tiers and make them more premium in look. Finally, the size of the labels was increased and embossed with a rich texture, providing an elegant finishing touch to the new upscale package design.

Edge, Fuse and Trim

LOCATION NAPA VALLEY, CALIFORNIA

Ray Signorello Jr. had a tough act to follow. In the mid-1970s, the Signorellos purchased a one-hundred-acre estate on the Silverado Trail, and on that foundation his father, Ray Sr., had built a sterling reputation as a producer of resplendent Bordeaux-style Cabernet Sauvignons. Like his father, Ray Jr. loved Cabernet Sauvignon, but he was eager to explore a bold new direction: to find exciting ways to introduce Cabernet Sauvignon to a whole new generation of wine drinkers, and do so at an affordable price.

EDGE WINES NAPA VALLEY, CALIFORNIA

Ray Signorello Jr. came to CF Napa looking for help in creating just the right look, feel and label for this new venture. He wanted to target those young wine aficionados who are always on the lookout for a new, contemporary red wine blend. In Ray's eyes, a classic Napa Valley Cabernet label would not suffice; he wanted to highlight his youthful approach and have the bottle stand out boldly on retailers' shelves. The name and premise here are clear: this is a cutting-edge, full-bodied, oak-aged Cabernet Sauvignon—without the stiff price of typical Napa Valley Cabs.

In terms of design, our approach came down to a single word: mystique. The Edge design concept makes no bow to the wine labels of old. In fact, there is almost no label at all, and there is no superfluous data to be found on the front label.

Instead, the presentation is stark and minimalist and almost without color—other than the three elegant red rings around the capsule and the bottom label where Napa Valley and Cabernet Sauvignon are called out in red. The main label is pared down to the brand name, Edge, written with no capital letter and cropped so tightly that it actually bleeds off the sleek black label. The brand name is printed in high-gloss silk screen, making it appear as if it cuts through directly to the glass of the bottle. The bottle was designed years prior by CF Napa for Demptos Glass but became the perfect selection for this new project with its reverse stair-step base that literally creates an edge on the bottle. The result is sleek and modern, exuding a palpable air of mystery and class.

2002 napa valley | cabernet sauvignon

FUSE WINES NAPA VALLEY, CALIFORNIA

Like his wine Edge, Ray Signorello's Fuse is a wine designed to appeal to the new generation of young urban wine drinkers. And this is a wine created with a daring and unusual twist–it is a classic Cabernet Sauvignon blended with a surprising partner: Syrah. This is a wine crafted to be bold and robust, hence the name Fuse.

To deliver the proper bang on the visual side, we stripped the design elements down to their essence and wrote out the name in bright red and rising upward, like a lit fuse ignited and ready to explode. The brand name straddles an organic texture embossed into the label, and the gap was printed in a high-gloss silk screen with only a few lines fusing

the two sides of the label together. The resulting effect makes it appear as if the label is made of two pieces, with the Fuse type floating on the bottle. Just for fun, the Fuse website features one of our earlier concepts: smoke curling upward from the wordmark, celebrating the wine's taste explosion and its youthful appeal.

Trim Wines California

Trim's tagline says it all: "Sophisticated Flavor, Sensible Value."

This is a lush, fruit-forward Cabernet Sauvignon aimed specifically at wine lovers from the millennial generation, one of the hottest segments of today's burgeoning wine market. And Trim offers something special: fruit sourced from a number of outstanding vineyards on California's prized North Coast. Five accomplished wine industry pros created Trim with one clear intention: to deliver a top-quality Cabernet Sauvignon at a very affordable price.

Our design for the branding and packaging is clean and modern. It makes use of two intersecting squares that seem to overlap one another. The first is a bright red square embossed with a toothy texture on an uncoated paper. The second is a contrasting glossy, smooth, gunmetal gray, foil stamped and overprinted with ink made to look like a glossy metallic second label. Then the brand name, Trim, was debossed into the label and stamped in a metallic foil to make it appear as if the brand name were die-cut through to the label below. The result creates a compelling optical illusion that is strong, clean and contemporary.

Fog Mountain

COMPANY   BOISSET FAMILY ESTATES, ST. HELENA, CALIFORNIA

APPELLATION   CALIFORNIA

In almost every aspect of the wine industry, Jean-Charles Boisset has been a fearless innovator. In his vineyards, he has aggressively pressed for biodynamic farming and the latest in organic methods, and as a creative marketer, Jean-Charles has few peers. He has also turned his revolutionary thinking to design and packaging, looking for ways to provide convenience and value for the wine consumer, while also developing new ways to protect the environment.

Fog Mountain is an illuminating case in point. Jean-Charles examined the process of producing, bottling, packaging and shipping wine to retailers, and he saw a glaring problem for the environment: glass. The glass used in traditional wine bottles uses a tremendous amount of natural resources and leaves a heavy carbon footprint. Instead of glass, Jean-Charles packaged his Fog Mountain

wine in a one-liter PET plastic bottle. Using this bottle produces a reduced carbon footprint, while delivering greater value and ease of use for the consumer.

With a name like Fog Mountain, we had many different options for the design and packaging. We explored different ways to convey the feeling of fog graphically, but most bordered on cliché. The solution we found creates the ethereal feeling of fog rolling off a hillside vineyard, and on close examination you see that the swirls of fog are made by the layering of the brand name many times over. We heightened the feeling of fog by rendering the image in a monochromatic mosaic of blues and purples. The graphic was then embossed to further accentuate the effect, creating a look that is visually arresting, yet elegantly simple.

FOG MOUNTAIN

2008

CALIFORNIA NOUVEAU

RED WINE

1 LITER

KITÁ

2010

CABERNET SAUVIGNON

Camp 4 Vineyard

SANTA BARBARA COUNTY ‖ SANTA YNEZ VALLEY

Kitá Wines

COMPANY   CHUMASH CELLARS, LLC, LOMPOC, CALIFORNIA

APPELLATION   SANTA YNEZ VALLEY, CALIFORNIA

The Chumash Indians bring a unique history to the world of wine. At one time, over twenty thousand Chumash lived in villages located on the Channel Islands and along the California coast between what are now Malibu and Monterey. Crushed by Spanish missionaries and American settlers, today only a small number of Chumash groups remain. The most prominent is the Santa Ynez Band of Chumash Indians, who reside in the Santa Barbara area and have thrived through astute ventures in tourism and agriculture, including the highly successful Chumash Casino Resort in Santa Ynez Valley.

In 2010, the Santa Ynez Band purchased fourteen hundred acres of land that they considered sacred ground—a Chumash community had been located there many generations before. Initially, Santa Ynez Band leaders planned to build housing on part of the property. Yet, the land had previously been owned by the Fess Parker Winery, and two hundred fifty acres of it were planted with premium grapes. After careful consideration, the Santa Ynez Band leaders decided to protect the land by retaining this exceptional vineyard and using it to launch a wine business of their own. They had the ideal person to run it: Tara Gomez, a Chumash descendent with extensive training and experience in wine and viticulture, including nearly a decade working as an enologist for J. Lohr Vineyards & Wines and making wine for her own label, Kalawashaq Wines.

In 2011, the Santa Ynez Band came to CF Napa for help with creating their new wine brand. Through historical research and a naming workshop with the band, we found a beautiful name, Kitá, which means "valley oak" in the Chumash's indigenous Samala language. The name also had special significance to the tribe. Their ancestors had lived off the natural bounties of the land, including the acorns of the valley oaks that thrived along the coast of California.

For the iconography, we looked for ways to portray the literal image as well as the deeper meanings of valley oaks for the Chumash tribe and culture. Our solution was an oak leaf icon that is constructed from concentric lines similar to the growth rings of an oak tree, to symbolize the many generations of the Chumash people and their proud heritage. The leaf was stamped in a pearl foil and then over-printed with a series of gold and silver inks and foils. The result is a jewel-like symbol that forms the centerpiece of the label design and also provides deep historic and symbolic significance to the entire brand.

Noval Black

COMPANY   QUINTA DO NOVAL, VILA NOVA DE GAIA, PORTUGAL
APPELLATION   DOURO VALLEY, PORTUGAL

Quinta do Noval is one of Portugal's oldest and most respected producers of fine Port wine. It has been in the business since 1715, producing a line of classic Ports for connoisseurs the world over. In 2006, though, Quinta do Noval brought forth something new and exciting from its vineyards in Portugal's Douro Valley. This was not a tawny or caramelized Port. Instead, it was a bold, velvety, fruit-forward Port designed to appeal to a whole new generation of consumers.

In the world of Port, this was a bold departure; it was even designed to be served slightly chilled. But how to present this new product in the US market? In the United Kingdom, wine drinkers are very well educated about Port. After all, British traders and entrepreneurs helped build the industry in Portugal. In the United States, though, very few consumers today are familiar with the history or the delights of Port. Quinta do Noval hoped its new product would reintroduce Port into the beverage consciousness of the American consumer, and generate substantial sales in the process.

Working with a team from Noval, we identified millennials as the optimum target market; these younger wine drinkers are driving much of today's import wine sales and are more open to exploring new wines and tastes. To reach them, our strategy was to create a Port brand that would look to consumers more like a cordial or a high-end spirit than a traditional Port. To capture this sensibility, we developed the name Noval Black, which sounded like a hip, contemporary name for a fine Scotch or cordial and also provided a nod to Noval's historic black raven icon.

To accentuate that message, we designed a custom glass bottle taller and sleeker than traditional Port bottles. The bottle was reminiscent of luxury cordials, but it retained Port's signature bulb in the neck of the bottle. The bottle was then finished with a cartouche of the raven incorporated into the black glass. The label itself is a simple, clean black square trimmed with a border of glossy black foil, framing the brand name in bright silver ink. The overall presentation is a stark black, reinforcing the name Noval Black and making it stand out boldly on the shelf. The Noval brand was first launched in New York, and since then it has caught fire across the US and internationally. And just as Quinta do Noval had hoped, Noval Black could be ushering in a whole new era in the history of Port.

PRESQU'ILE

PINOT NOIR
SANTA MARIA VALLEY
VINTAGE 2008

Presqu'ile

COMPANY   PRESQU'ILE WINERY, SANTA MARIA, CALIFORNIA
APPELLATION   SANTA MARIA VALLEY, CALIFORNIA

One of the biggest movements in US wine today is toward sustainability. This refers to farming practices designed to grow grapes in ways that are as natural as possible, sensitive to the environment and repeatable year after year. For many wineries, sustainability is a relatively new concept, but not at the Presqu'ile Winery. In their idyllic setting on California's Central Coast and in their native Louisiana, the Murphy family has been involved in sustainable farming, forestry and environmental protection for more than a century. And their work has earned national recognition. In 2004 the family was honored with the coveted National Wetlands Conservation Award for their work in restoring wetlands in Louisiana.

At Presqu'ile, their two-hundred-acre estate in the Santa Maria Valley, the Murphys have created a model of sustainable grape growing and wine-making. Presqu'ile uses no herbicides or pesticides in its vineyards. To enrich the soil, the Murphys use nitrogen-fixing and flowering cover crops. To attract beneficial insect predators, they promote the growth of clover and wildflowers, and they make special efforts to preserve the natural habitats of coyotes, foxes, bobcats, owls, bats, red-tailed hawks, falcons and other natural predators. For

the Murphys, it is all about living in partnership with nature–and with their local community. To that end, the Murphys provide needs-based college and vocational scholarships, and they encourage their staff to volunteer with the charities of their choice.

CF Napa worked with Presqu'ile's marketing team to define the brand's essence and to develop its story. The word *presqu'ile* is French for "peninsula" or literally "almost an island," and for the Murphys it refers back to their family property on the Gulf Coast, a sanctuary where they often spent summer days relaxing, sailing and swimming. In 2005, though, the family home and property were totally destroyed by Hurricane Katrina. To pay tribute to those roots and to tie them to the Murphys' winery, we created a design that evokes the sense of their family home with a graphic abstract of sails, representing the wind and water they enjoyed during summer days together. There is an underlying tension here: the same wind and water that can be horrifically destructive, as they were in Katrina, are essential for cultivating beautiful grapes for wine. Such is the power of Mother Nature, and such is the importance of working in harmony with her.

Bacio Divino Cellars

LOCATION OAKVILLE, NAPA VALLEY, CALIFORNIA

Claus Janzen is a dreamer, a rebel, a music lover, an accomplished photographer and a man who is not comfortable unless he is breaking rules and pushing the conventional boundaries of wine, art and life itself. His wines and their names express that spirit. One is called Vagabond. Another is Bacio Divino (meaning "divine kiss" in Italian), and still another is called Pazzo (Italian for "crazy").

PAZZO OAKVILLE, NAPA VALLEY, CALIFORNIA

The story of Claus's Pazzo tells you a lot about the man. Pazzo followed on the heels of Bacio Divino, a divine blend of Cabernet Sauvignon and Sangiovese. That wine was an immediate success, and Claus was eager to follow it with a series of other unusual, consumer-friendly blends. Eager to break with any and all tradition, Claus played around and came up with an unpretentious wine that blended some very exotic partners: Sangiovese, Cabernet, Zinfandel, Merlot and Viognier.

Claus came to CF Napa looking for a label and packaging that would be as equally zany and vivacious as the wine itself. His only instruction to us was, "Go crazy!" And we did. Using a color palette of vivid yellow and red, we developed a mesmerizing spiral, with the letter P written at the very center. Then, to accentuate the vertigo effect, we made everything on the package off-kilter, from the angles of the label to the cut of the capsule on top. The final touch was a hand-drawn wordmark for the brand inspired by Alfred Hitchcock's *Vertigo*.

JANZEN OAKVILLE, NAPA VALLEY, CALIFORNIA

When Claus Janzen set out to create a line of luxury Cabernet
Sauvignons, wines selling at seventy-five dollars and more,
he wanted to avoid the usual stodgy, classic labels of Napa Valley
that were inspired by the French tradition. Instead, Claus wanted
a label that stood out dramatically from the crowd, a label
that was modern and edgy, like his wine Pazzo, but also a label
and package that exuded the ultimate in extravagance and class.
These wines would be made from some of finest grapes grown in
the Napa Valley, including Claus's own estate vineyard and Andy
Beckstoffer's To Kalon Vineyard, one of the most esteemed
vineyards in the Napa Valley.

For inspiration, we turned to some of the great masters of modern
art, to painters like Robert Motherwell, Jackson Pollock and Joan
Miró. The look we created strikes a balance between frenzied
modernity and high-polished elegance. The line graphic on the
left forms a sharp, chaotic signature. Here we relied on the style
of gestural drawings, with the goal of conveying Claus's spirit
of "impulsive creativity." The only other information on the front
label is the brand name, Janzen, set in calm juxtaposition to the
lines and debossed into beautifully textured paper. The result is a
label of distinction and dramatic simplicity, a symbol of fine art,
just like the wine itself.

PHOTO RIGHT: *Janzen To Kalon Vineyard*

Hanna

COMPANY   Terlato Wines International, Lake Bluff, Illinois
and Hanna Winery & Vineyards, Healdsburg, California

APPELLATION   Russian River Valley & Alexander Valley, Sonoma County, California

Dr. Elias S. Hanna, a world-renowned cardiac surgeon, was born and raised in the countryside of Syria. His family grew a variety of crops, including grapes, and early on young Elias came to see his family vineyard as a place of tranquility and promise, a soil in which dreams could be planted and would naturally grow. After he moved to San Francisco and established his busy practice, Dr. Hanna needed a sanctuary, an anchor in the soil, a place where he could return to the land and cultivate grapes.

Dr. Hanna found his sanctuary in Sonoma County. In the 1970s, he purchased twelve acres in the Russian River Valley, and there he and his children began handcrafting their own wines, Chardonnay and Cabernet Sauvignon. But that was just the beginning. Soon Dr. Hanna hired a professional winemaker and expanded his holdings to over six hundred acres in Sonoma County, spread over four different vineyards. For the past twenty years, his daughter Christine has run the Hanna Winery and Vineyards.

In 2006 Hanna Winery and Terlato Wines, Hanna's sales and marketing company, came to CF Napa with a classic problem: the wines they were crafting, especially their Sauvignon Blanc, were of exceptional quality, but their label was outdated, and they worried it was affecting sales. We agreed. Their existing label had a color palette that could best be described as Victorian, featuring a dark

green and red, both presented on a butter yellow background. This was not a particularly refreshing look and certainly not in line with the competition's more contemporary packaging. Also, their original label had a geometric stair-step shape that proved to be exceptionally difficult for the winery to apply correctly on the bottle. The label had won some design awards in the past, but we found no clear rationale or visible connection to the estate. Still, the odd shape was memorable, and Hanna and Terlato had worries about tampering with what was one of the stronger equity elements of the packaging.

As part of the exploration we looked at different ways to maintain that unusual shape. Ultimately, though, we all agreed on a complete overhaul, using a more traditional label shape that vastly facilitated the bottling and labeling process. A new icon was developed using wildflowers as the subject matter, and the wordmark was evolved with a completely new color system palette that was warm, rural and friendly, just like Sonoma County itself. The new colors also highlighted the wine's flavor cues of citrus and grapefruit. The wordmark for Hanna was then printed in a lush, feminine, persimmon color with a capsule to match. With the packaging finally descriptive of the wine inside, sales for the brand immediately soared.

DEMETRIA

2005

Pinot Noir

STA. RITA HILLS

GAIA VINEYARD

Demetria

COMPANY   DEMETRIA ESTATE, LOS OLIVOS, CALIFORNIA
APPELLATION   SANTA YNEZ VALLEY, CALIFORNIA

John Zahoudanis was born and raised in a small Greek village at the foot of historic Mount Olympus. His family had a long tradition in agriculture, and for generations they cultivated their own vineyards and made their own wines. But two wars brought all that to a nasty end. When John was a boy, the family farm was devastated by World War II and then by the Greek Civil War. His vineyards ruined, John's father relocated the entire family to the US. John spent the remainder of his childhood in Colorado, and later he had a successful career in commercial real estate. But John's love of fine wine never ebbed, and he and his wife, Sandra, often made tasting trips to California Wine Country and to the winegrowing regions of France.

In 2005 John and Sandra finally took the plunge. They purchased a beautiful property in the rolling hills of the Santa Ynez Valley in Santa Barbara County, and there they started their own wine company, Demetria Estate. Like John's childhood home in Greece, the Demetria Estate has a Mediterranean feel and is ideally situated for growing top-quality grapes. John and Sandra, hands-on owners, now produce a small line of biodynamically grown wines.

For brand packaging, John came to CF Napa. Inspired by his Greek heritage, we fashioned the label to feature a decorative border constructed from a continuous line known as the Greek Key, a motif that has been used through the ages by the Greeks and can be found on centuries-old Greek and Roman pottery. In our search for a central icon, we discovered that many Greek coins, beginning in Roman times, featured a ram's head on the face of the coin—we had our inspiration. For the icon, we created a symbol composed of two interlocking rams' heads representing Demetria Estate's two prized vineyards, one inland and one coastal. The icon also alludes to the winery's commitment to biodynamic farming, drawing together the core elements of nature, vines and the artistry of the winemaker.

Boneshaker

COMPANY Hahn Family Wines, Napa, California
APPELLATION Lodi, California

Boneshaker, the latest addition to Hahn Family Wines' Cycles Gladiator line of wines, is a big, bold Zinfandel. The name traces back to the nickname given to Velocipedes, a line of early bicycles from the Golden Age of Cycling (1860–1905). Those bicycles were originally made entirely of wood–metal tires were added later–making for a thrilling but incredibly bumpy ride across the cobblestones of the day. In fact, those early bikes rattled their riders so badly that they came to be known infamously as "boneshakers."

The parodies of that day often featured skeletons on bikes, a salute to the riders' bone-shaking experience, and this became our inspiration for the wine's imagery. Instead of using a full skeleton, we designed the label with a single iconic skull. Presented in bone white on a midnight black background, the starkness of the label reinforces the bold style of the Zinfandel. Viewed from afar, the image reads clearly as a skull, but when you take a closer look, you see that the skull is built from the typography of the label and various parts of bicycles; the wheels of the Velocipede itself form the eyes of the skull. As a final touch, we printed the label with glow-in-the-dark ink, so that when viewed in complete darkness the haunting image of the skull glows right back at you. It is an image guaranteed to shake your bones!

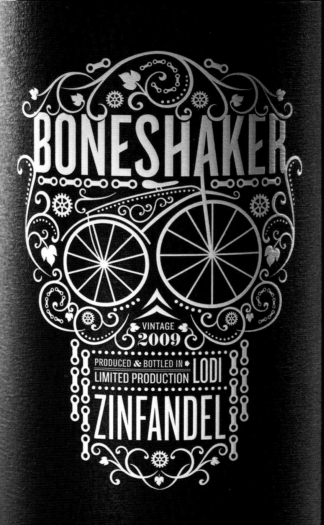

BONESHAKER

VINTAGE
2009

PRODUCED & BOTTLED IN ❧ LODI
LIMITED PRODUCTION

ZINFANDEL

Kesner

COMPANY   KESNER WINES, HEALDSBURG, CALIFORNIA
APPELLATION   NORTH COAST, CALIFORNIA

Jason Kesner is a purist, a winemaker who believes in letting nature reign supreme. That means low-impact farming and low-impact winemaking too. At Kesner Wines, there is no manipulation of the wine through additions of yeast, acid or bacteria. All the wines are aged on their lees, then racked and blended only once before bottling, to preserve the distinctive characters of each barrel. Jason uses no set schedules or formulas for crafting his wines. He believes the wine and its evolution should be guided by the particular quality and character of the fruit–and nothing else.

Jason's label is likewise natural and elegant in its simplicity. A contemporary, abstract *K* makes up the main graphic on the label, giving way to pristine white space and elegantly organized type. The result exudes a Zen-like sense of balance, reflecting Jason's method of winemaking. The quality of the wine and branding has paid off handsomely. When Jason presented his inaugural Sonoma Coast Chardonnay to some of the finest restaurants in the country, star chef Thomas Keller was so impressed that he made it a highly recommended choice on his wine list at The French Laundry–an honor that Jason's wine has earned with every vintage since.

Ansted & Co.

COMPANY   ANSTED & CO., VICTORIA, AUSTRALIA
APPELLATION   HARCOURT VALLEY, BENDIGO, AUSTRALIA

Tobias Ansted started working in the wine industry when he was still in high school near Canberra, Australia. He then studied wine science at Charles Sturt University and later went on to hone his winemaking skills at different wineries in Argentina and in the Loire Valley, Burgundy, and the Languedoc region in France.

In 2000 Tobias returned home to Australia, eager to turn his skills into high art. Three years later, he planted his own vineyard in the lovely Harcourt Valley, south of Bendigo, Victoria, and northwest of Melbourne. For his own wines, Tobias had two guiding values: quality and creative freedom, and he set out to create limited quantities of single-vineyard wines that would beautifully express the character, soil and climate of the Harcourt Valley. His first wine was a Syrah, but in 2012 he added a fresh white wine made from the Rhône varietals Marsanne and Viognier.

When Tobias came to CF Napa, he spoke eloquently about how the best wines are always the result of three elements working harmoniously together: the vineyard workers, the cellar workers, and the hands of Mother Nature herself. The challenge was to capture Tobias's story and uplifting values on a single label. The solution features a striking woodcut illustration of three birds converging in flight, symbolizing those three essential elements that must come together to produce the finest of wines. The rich textural quality of the woodcut adds a distinctive sensory dimension to the label, embodying the soaring elegance of Tobias's vision and values and of the lovely qualities of the wine inside the bottle.

ANSTED&CO.
SYRAH
ANSTED&CO.
NORTH HARCOURT VINEYARD
SYRAH
ANSTED&CO.
NORTH HARCOURT VINEYARD
SYRAH

2007
RUSSIAN RIVER VALLEY
PINOT NOIR

J VINEYARDS

J Vineyards & Winery

COMPANY J Vineyards & Winery, Healdsburg, California
APPELLATION Russian River Valley, California

With Judy Jordan, wine runs deep in her genes. Her father, Tom Jordan, founded the Jordan Vineyard & Winery back in 1972, and he earned a glowing reputation as one of the true pioneers of Sonoma County wine. Judy seemed to be made for success in no matter what field she chose to pursue. A star tennis player and athlete, she went to Stanford, studied geology and earth science, and after graduation she worked hard to develop her expertise in business, marketing, geology and soils.

Wine was the obvious next step. In 1986 Judy launched her own wine company, now called J Vineyards & Winery. From the outset, she crafted critically acclaimed sparkling wines, but she soon realized that her vineyards would also be ideal for producing site-specific, cool-climate Russian River Valley varietal wines like Pinot Noir, Chardonnay and Pinot Gris. Along with making beautiful wines, Judy brought a special elegance and flair to her winery. In fact, *Sunset* magazine named her Healdsburg winery "The Best Tasting Room in the West."

In designing her labels, we took our inspiration from one of Judy's passions: geology. We explored the avulsion (river bed movement) of the Russian River and the strata of the alluvial soils of gravel, loam and sandy soils found along the river valley that were transported to the area by the river's ever-changing path. These incredible soils provide the rich characteristics of the wines grown in the famed Russian River Valley. The label design makes use of the lines that are debossed into the label, creating a richly textural, yet modern representation of the land's geology and stratum. The iconic paint stroke *J* icon created by CF Napa many years earlier was then incorporated with clean, simple type, allowing the texture to help tell the story of the vineyards that give birth to their wines.

Domenichelli

COMPANY   DOMENICHELLI WINES, CLOVERDALE, CALIFORNIA
APPELLATION   MENDOCINO COUNTY, CALIFORNIA

As Steve Domenichelli explains, wine is "in my family's bloodstream." His great grandfather, Remigio Domenichelli, emigrated from northern Italy to Geyserville, in California Wine Country. On his ranch there, Remigio grew grapes and started his own winery. When Prohibition hit, however, Remigio closed his business. He never reopened it, and that could have been the end of the story.

Remigio and his wife, Felicina, had seven sons, and all seven loved the country life, with good food and wine, farming, fishing and mushroom hunting. But none of the sons chose to devote his life to wine. To make his mark in the US, Steve's grandfather, Willy, went into real estate, often dealing in ranches and vineyards, but his son William proved that wine was still in the family bloodstream. William loved growing grapes and making wine, and this passion was eventually passed on to his son, Steve.

As a boy, Steve Domenichelli worked alongside his father, growing prunes, pears and grapes, and when he was older, Steve went to work managing other vineyards in Sonoma County and the Russian River Valley. But when Steve had his own children, they often asked about the family's passionate history in wine and viticulture. Ultimately, Steve

and his wife, Stephanie, decided to create a special line of wines to honor his father and to celebrate Steve's great grandfather, Remigio, and the seven original Domenichelli brothers. They named the wine Magnificent 7.

For CF Napa, the challenge was to create a look that expressed luxury and elegance but could also be affordably produced at exceptionally low quantities. The design we developed uses an intricate Italian pattern inspired by the classic patterns found in Italian artwork and fabric. Against a stark black background, the brand name Domenichelli appears in crisp white, thus jumping right out to the eye. Underneath, the brand name Magnificent 7 appears in a discreet red, along with the varietal and the vintage year. The labels were digitally printed as an affordable solution to their low production and a way to accommodate the variable case production and winemaking notes on each of the front labels. The savings were then reallocated to accomplish the laser die-cut pattern that acts as the brand's primary graphic. The result is incredibly intricate with a high-touch feel, making the label look and feel as handcrafted as the wines themselves.

DOMENICHELLI

MAGNIFICENT 7 | ZINFANDEL

2005

BLUEBIRD
PINOT NOIR

CALIFORNIA 20
09

Bluebird (bloo'bŭrd') *n.* - not a bird, instead a long
sunny day perfect for playing in the mountains.

BLUEBIRD
CABERNET
SAUVIGNON

NORTH COAST 20
07

Bluebird (bloo'bŭrd') *n.* - not a bird, instead a long
sunny day perfect for playing in the mountains.

Bluebird

COMPANY   HOME TEAM WINES, SONOMA, CALIFORNIA, AND X WINERY, NAPA, CALIFORNIA
APPELLATION   CALIFORNIA

Bluebird began as a collaboration between the partners of Home Team Wines–Ryan Donnelly and Lane Shackleton–and the founder of X Winery, Reed Renaudin. These young entrepreneurs envisioned Bluebird as a fun, enjoyable and affordable tribute to "the good life," California-style, meaning good times shared outdoors with family and friends. They chose the brand name, Bluebird, for its slang usage connoting those spectacular sunny days when the world is so alive that we all feel that the possibilities are endless.

These young wine enthusiasts also had a higher purpose: They wanted to promote sustainable grape farming and the use of environmentally sensitive production methods. The design and packaging were to follow suit, bringing fresh, creative ideas to the world of wine. To convey the right feeling of youth and innovation, a hand-drawn typeface was combined with a woodcut illustration of a sunny mountain landscape. The paper label is debossed to give it a rich, textured letter-pressed feel, and the blue monochromatic color scheme reinforces the brand name while clearly setting it apart from competitors. But that was just the beginning.

After the launch of Bluebird, CF Napa was approached by AstraPouch, a company producing a new earth-friendly alternative to traditional wine packaging. The pitch was compelling: Glass bottles are heavy, cumbersome, breakable and expensive to ship. Glass, furthermore, is not well suited for today's active outdoor lifestyles; who wants to tuck a clunky bottle into a backpack or beach bag? In terms of the environment, glass presents other concerns: used bottles fill our landfills; producing glass generates loads of greenhouse gasses; and massive amounts of fossil fuels are needed to transport heavy pallets loaded with glass bottles. The new AstraPouch, by contrast, is light, portable and virtually unbreakable. The potential for the Bluebird brand to leverage this new format was clear.

The Bluebird-AstraPouch union augments Bluebird's sustainable and active lifestyle positioning. A single Bluebird pouch holds the same amount of wine as two traditional bottles–at a fraction of the weight. And because it collapses after usage, the pouch produces 70 percent less landfill and uses a full 80 percent fewer greenhouse gasses to produce. Moreover, unlike a bottle, if you only want to drink a glass or two of the wine, the pouch closes air-tight, preventing oxidation and the ruin of the taste.

PHOTO LEFT: *Bluebird Pinot Noir & Cabernet Sauvignon*
PHOTO ABOVE LEFT: *Bluebird Pinot Noir AstraPouch*
PHOTO ABOVE RIGHT: *Bluebird Pinot Noir*

La Merika

COMPANY   DELICATO FAMILY VINEYARDS, NAPA, CALIFORNIA
APPELLATION   CENTRAL COAST, CALIFORNIA

Gasparé Indelicato is one of the great untold stories of American wine. He grew up in the village of Campobello, on the western coast of Sicily, where his father, his grandfather, his great grandfather and even their fathers had all made bright, fresh Mediterranean wines. Eager to branch out on his own, Gasparé emigrated to the US, and he landed happily in California's sun-bathed San Joaquin Valley. In 1924, some ninety years ago, Gasparé planted the very first grapes for what became Delicato Family Vineyards. And in that same soil, Gasparé also planted his most cherished values: Honesty. Decency. Trust. Generosity. Family.

With those values, Gasparé steered his family business through the dark days of Prohibition, and his sons and grandsons have continued to carry his torch right to the present day, making the Indelicatos one of the leading family winegrowers in the US. At Delicato Family Vineyards and its subsidiary, Coastal Wine Brands, the family makes a wide variety of fresh, honest, affordable wines sourced from vineyards up and down the state of California. With grapes from the Central Coast, they created La Merika as a special tribute to Gasparé and his heritage and values.

The brand name, La Merika, refers to a star in the western sky, one that, according to legend, many European explorers relied on when they sailed for the New World. Accordingly, our package design contains elements from the maps and charts of those ancient explorers, embellished by a central icon crafted from a compass rose. The label is embossed with a cartographic texture that creates a wake in the symbolic water behind the icon and points to the star on the far left side of the label. The resulting label and iconography are a fitting tribute to those ancient mariners and, above all, to the pioneering spirit of Gasparé Indelicato.

LA MERIKA

2009 | PINOT NOIR
CENTRAL COAST

THE CLIMBER
RED WINE
2009
CALIFORNIA
CLIF FAMILY WINERY
THE CLIMBER
CHARDONNAY
CALIFORNIA
CLIF FAMILY WINERY
80% LOWER CARBON FOOTPRINT
90% LESS WASTE THAN GLASS
1.5L
2 x 750ML BOTTLES

The Climber

COMPANY   CLIF FAMILY WINERY, ST. HELENA, CALIFORNIA
APPELLATION   CALIFORNIA

Gary Erickson is a man who follows his passions, including cycling, the outdoors, good wine and eating healthy, nutritious food. All of these passions merged with the creation of The Climber.

In 1990 midway through a one-day, 175-mile bicycle ride, and after one too many sticky, unpleasant energy bars, Gary had what he calls "the epiphany." He was convinced that he could create an energy bar that was both healthy and tasty, and soon the CLIF Bar was born. Named for his father, Clifford, the CLIF Bar was launched in 1992 and became an instant hit with cyclists and climbers. Together with his partner and co-owner and CEO, Kit Crawford, Gary has grown the company into one of the US's most prominent producers of organic energy bars and drinks, with a very loyal following among environmentally minded consumers.

On the wings of this success, Gary and Kit purchased a home and farm in the Napa Valley, which then led to a new creative adventure for the pair: the Clif Family Winery. Kit shares Gary's love of good food and wine, and this combined with another shared interest in sustainable farming made winemaking a natural next step for them both. Yet, Gary and Kit had a complex branding challenge. How would they transfer the fabulous success of their CLIF Bar to their new line of wines? At a practical level, should the CLIF Bar logo continue to be integrated into the branding and packaging for their wines?

In our experience, the wine industry is something of a world unto itself; successful brands outside the wine business do not readily translate into successful wine brands. For instance, in the case of CLIF, the brand's success in organic energy and nutritional foods and drinks did not provide automatic credibility in the wine business. Accordingly, we changed the hierarchy of their brand's name from CLIF to the more fanciful name, The Climber, to cement the core linkage between active lifestyle consumers, their deep love of the outdoor life and Clif Family Winery's wine brand. The strategy worked.

Gary and Kit launched the brand in glass bottles to great success, and soon we introduced them to the new green alternative for wine packaging, the AstraPouch. Light and ultraportable, the pouch is perfect for those on the go. For campers, hikers or those simply heading to the beach, the pouch functions far better than glass and is far easier on the environment. AstraPouch proved an ideal fit for the brand's key demographic and positioning.

Joseph Phelps Vineyards

LOCATION St. Helena, California

Joseph Phelps is a legend in the Napa Valley. In Colorado, he built one of the largest construction companies in the US, and then he fell in love with the art of wine. In 1973 Joe came to California and found a jewel: a six-hundred-acre cattle ranch outside the town of St. Helena, in the northern part of the Napa Valley. He bought the property, planted vineyards and began producing what would eventually become several of the valley's most sought-after fine wines. Over the years, CF Napa has designed many of the Joseph Phelps labels, including its main line of wines, its ice wine Eisrébe, its single-vineyard red wine Backus, and its iconic red wine, Insignia.

BACKUS Oakville, Napa Valley, California

The Backus Vineyard is a glorious, sun-swept vineyard along the Silverado Trail, boasting iron-rich soil and steeply terraced vineyards. When we began working on the project, we learned that there was a historic smokehouse standing in the middle of the vineyard, a weathered building with walls of rugged stone and a copper roof. That smokehouse became the main icon for the brand. To firmly establish it, we used historic land deeds and a sepia-toned photograph of the old smokehouse as the central imagery. To augment the impact, we created a high "touch factor," using richly textured paper and a debossed printing that harkens back to the classic letterpress printing process in which the ink was pressed into the paper with metal type. The result is a label of refinement and distinction, perfectly suited for this exceptional wine.

Backus

NAPA VALLEY
OAKVILLE
CABERNET SAUVIGNON

1999

BOTTLE No. 4279

JOSEPH PHELPS
VINEYARDS

JOSEPH PHELPS

V I N E Y A R D S

Cabernet Sauvignon

NAPA VALLEY

VINTAGE 2000

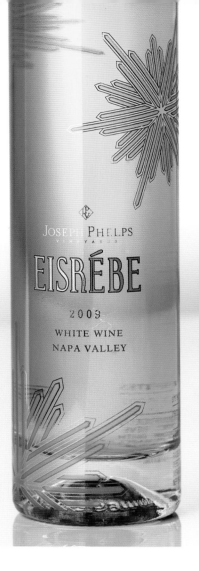

Joseph Phelps Napa Valley, California

For the Phelps' main tier of wines, we commissioned an engraving-like illustration that captures the beauty of the family's secluded valley estate. We then created a stately JPV logo that would tie together the wines underneath the Joseph Phelps brand and create a uniform brand connection across the line.

Eisrébe Napa Valley, California

Great vintners like Joe Phelps are constantly innovating and experimenting. In that spirit, his team set out to create something new for the Napa Valley: an "ice wine," or *Eiswein*, as it is called in Germany. Ice wine is popular in cold climates like Canada, but this was a major departure for the Napa Valley. Ice wine is a type of dessert wine produced from grapes that have frozen while still on the vine, resulting in a very sweet wine of concentrated character and flavor. To make theirs, in the much warmer climate of the Napa Valley, the specialists at Joseph Phelps picked their grapes late in the season and then carefully froze them to produce the highly concentrated flavors and sugar levels characteristic of ice wines.

In designing the package, we chose a tall flint, or clear, bottle to highlight the wine's rich golden color, and then we embellished the glass using a silk-screening process applied directly to the bottle. This technique allowed the wine to show through the design. To convey a wintery feel, we created crystal-like snowflakes, crafted in gold foil with frosted etching. The wordmark recalls the wine's Germanic heritage and was hand-drawn based on the celebrated art nouveau font Eckmann, designed by the German painter and graphic artist Otto Eckmann (1865–1902). The overall effect created is that of snowflakes gently drifting across the bottle, hinting at the process that produces this fabulous ice wine.

PHOTO LEFT: *Joseph Phelps Main Tier*
PHOTO RIGHT: *Eisrébe*

INSIGNIA NAPA VALLEY, CALIFORNIA

Insignia has an impressive pedigree. Soon after he started his winery, Joseph Phelps set out to make a Bordeaux-style blend of the highest quality, a wine that could stand proudly next to the very best wines from Pauillac, Margaux or Saint-Émilion. The result was Insignia, the first proprietary Bordeaux-style blend produced in California. And Joe's Insignia quickly fulfilled its promise: it is a big, bold, opulent wine, one of the highest expressions of California's glorious grapes and winemaking artistry.

Today, nearly forty years after its inaugural vintage, Insignia is still hailed as one of the great wines of the world. The 2002 vintage was awarded "Wine of the Year" by the *Wine Spectator*, and the 2009 Insignia marked the twentieth consecutive vintage to earn a ninety-plus score from Robert Parker's *The Wine Advocate*. And the quality keeps rising. Today each vintage of this Cabernet Sauvignon-based blend is crafted exclusively from six Phelps' estate vineyards located throughout the Napa Valley. The result is an American wine legend.

For this historic wine, we started by developing a custom bottle design with broad shoulders and a distinctive foot. The bottle has an inset panel in the glass that cradles the label. The label design is simple and clean and makes use of a rich, entwining pattern of grape leaves. This pattern was inspired by the prints of William Morris, an English textile designer whose work first gained prominence during the late 1880s. The design is crowned by an elegant insignia: a Cabernet Sauvignon leaf embellished in gold foil. The result is a proud, stately design, as befits this revered Napa Valley icon.

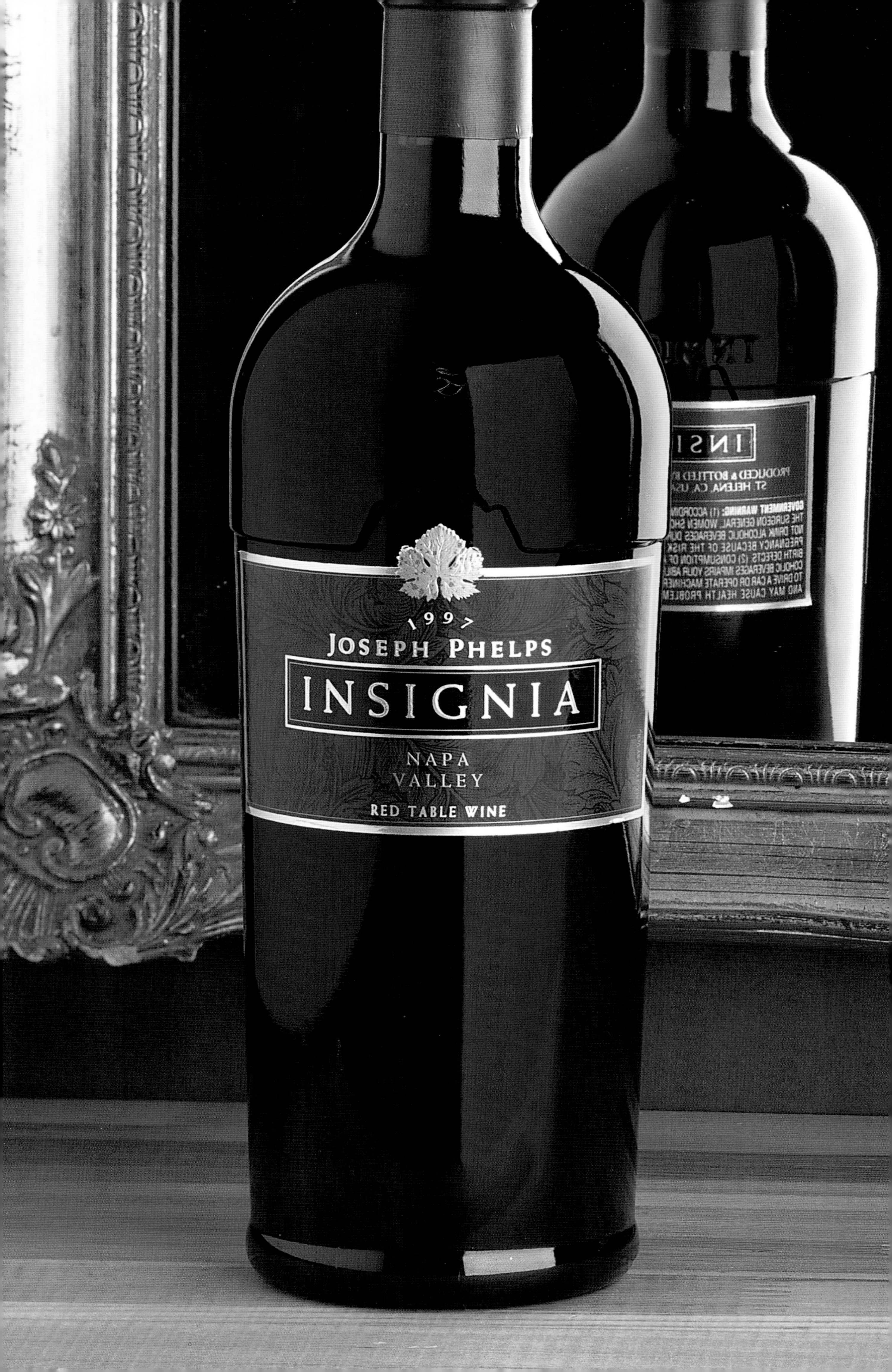
1997
JOSEPH PHELPS
INSIGNIA
NAPA
VALLEY
RED TABLE WINE

2010
ALAKAI
CALIFORNIA
RED WINE
JOEL GOTT
CELLARED AND BOTTLED BY JOEL GOTT WINES
ST. HELENA, NAPA COUNTY, CA ALC 14.4% BY VOLUME

Alakai

COMPANY JOEL GOTT WINES, ST. HELENA, CALIFORNIA
APPELLATION CALIFORNIA

Joel Gott is a restless spirit and an incessant creator. He hails
from a family that has been in the wine business for five
generations. When Joel was a boy, his parents hauled him from
one winery to another, cultivating in him a deep love of good
wine and food. After high school, Joel apprenticed to Mike Lee,
the wine master at Kenwood Vineyards in Sonoma County,
and in 1996 Joel launched his own brand. Since then, Joel has
developed strong relationships with many of the top Californian
grape growers, whose fruit has allowed him to bring forth
a range of delicious, well-crafted and affordable wines.

Joel's inspiration for the name Alakai was twofold: the high
plateau rainforest in Kauai, one of the few places where you
can walk in the clouds, and Joel's wife's cherished and longtime
vineyard dog, Alakai. For the design he sought a label with
elegant typography that was simple, yet a bit eclectic. The
solution makes use of a sky of cloud-white, toothy paper that
acts as a rich backdrop for the highly crafted typography
of the label. The Alakai wordmark is set in a deep black that is
raised in a silk screen and embossed. The hierarchy of the label
was intentionally designed to feel a bit eccentric, with the large
vintage date influenced by European wine labels, putting just
the right final touch to this modern classic.

DeLoach Vineyards

COMPANY DeLoach Vineyards, Santa Rosa, California

APPELLATION Russian River Valley, California

DeLoach Vineyards has a rich history in California wine. Founded in 1975, DeLoach immediately became a pioneering force in the Russian River Valley, producing high-quality, artisanal Pinot Noirs in one of California's premier winegrowing regions. The DeLoach brand languished, though–until the arrival of the creative, flamboyant Frenchman, Jean-Charles Boisset. In 2003 Jean-Charles bought DeLoach and brought it under his family collection of wineries, Boisset Family Estates. Then Jean-Charles and his teams went to work. With major investment, he upgraded the DeLoach vineyards, implementing organic and biodynamic farming methods, and expanded its single-vineyard program. His goal was to reestablish DeLoach as one of the Russian River's preeminent producers of top-quality Pinot Noir wines.

Jean-Charles brought in CF Napa to assess the brand's different tiers of wine and to find ways to restore the brand to its earlier stature. The process was revealing. In the wine industry, certain hidden cues in packaging tell the consumer that a given wine is both handcrafted and high-quality. Those cues create "pull" and stimulate sales. We found that the DeLoach packaging lacked these appropriate cues. From there we zeroed in on refurbishing the brand's historic French cachet and on better highlighting its equity symbol, the fleur-de-lis, to help consumers find the brand on crowded retail shelves.

As a first step, we refined and enlarged the fleur-de-lis icon and gave it more dimensionality by using gold foil, a sculptured emboss and a bronze ink overprint. Then we enhanced the quality cues by adding subtle design elements, including richly textured paper, visual depth and details of the brand story on the front label. Once the label had the needed class and sophistication, sales soon quadrupled, a dramatic example of how the label and packaging can affect the way consumers perceive a wine brand and ultimately augment sales.

PHOTO ABOVE LEFT: *DeLoach Reserve Tier*
PHOTO ABOVE RIGHT: *DeLoach Vineyard Designate*
PHOTO RIGHT: *DeLoach Main Tier*

DE LOACH
V I N E Y A R D S

2008

Russian River Valley

PINOT NOIR

Open-top Vat Fermentation

NESTLED IN THE HEART OF SONOMA COUNTY, DELOACH VINEYARDS OFFERS A UNIQUE
BLEND OF BURGUNDIAN WINEMAKING HERITAGE AND RUSSIAN RIVER VALLEY TERROIR

A FAMILY TRADITION SINCE 1975

PARALLEL

CABERNET SAUVIGNON 20
NAPA VALLEY 03

Parallel

COMPANY   PARALLEL WINES, NAPA, CALIFORNIA
APPELLATION   NAPA VALLEY, CALIFORNIA

Parallel Wines had an unusual birth. In June 1999 three couples, all of them friends from Park City, Utah, happened to be visiting Napa Valley at the same time. The couples fell in love with the valley, and their imaginations started to soar. As real estate professionals, their focus soon turned to purchasing a vineyard of their own, and before long they were joint owners of a beautiful property in Napa Valley.

A few months later in Park City, after a glorious day out on the slopes, the owners gathered for a dinner to decide on the name for their forthcoming wine brand. The name would connect their Park City roots, longtime friendship and common interest in wine and skiing. Soon they arrived at the perfect name: Parallel, a ski term that also represents their parallel passions.

At CF Napa, we love bringing forth the back stories that reveal the spirit of a winemaker or owner and that help give each brand its distinctive character and feel. The essence of those stories can then be communicated through the label and packaging. And so it was with Parallel. To convey the parallel interests and passions of the brand owners, our design team started with those parallel tracks that skiers leave in fresh mountain snow. On the label, the parallel lines elegantly intersect, giving it the look and feel of modern art. With its clean, crisp lines and stark black-and-white composition, the label takes on a true iconic stature. To provide a contrasting, irreverent touch, the bottle features a signature yellow capsule, suggesting the warm sun shining down on those ski slopes and on the abiding friendship of Parallel's partners.

Index

LISTED BY COMPANY NAME

About the Author

DAVID SCHUEMANN is the Owner and Creative Director of CF Napa Brand Design. He earned his BFA in Graphic Design at the University of Wisconsin–Eau Claire and started his career shortly after in Minneapolis, Minnesota, where he worked for the US record label K-Tel Records and later Carlson Marketing Group, one of the largest ad agencies in the world. Early in his career David fell in love with wine while working at many restaurants as a wine trainer and server; at that time he also became an avid personal collector. In 2000 Schuemann moved to San Francisco and joined Addison Branding as its Design Director. There he oversaw packaging and large corporate identity projects, including the complete rebranding of Hawaiian Airlines and its fleet of airplanes. Soon thereafter, Schuemann found the perfect marriage of his passions for wine and design, becoming the Creative Director for CF Napa Brand Design and a few years later purchasing the firm.

Over the past decade, Schuemann has led CF Napa Brand Design to become one of the world's preeminent brand agencies specializing in wine, spirits and beer. During that time, CF Napa has created some of the fastest-growing and most successful brands in the world. The firm's work has earned international recognition from almost every major design competition in the world and has been showcased in some of the most prestigious museums, including the Museum of Modern Art. CF Napa's work is part of the permanent collection at the Cooper Hewitt Design Museum at the Smithsonian in New York City, and the permanent collection of the American Design Archives at the Denver Art Museum.

ABOUT THE FOREWORD AUTHOR

AGUSTIN HUNEEUS SR. has been dedicated to the wine business for over fifty years. He has run wine companies in Chile, Argentina, Spain, France, Italy, Germany, New Zealand and California and created such renowned wine brands as Quintessa, Estancia, Magnificat, Veramonte, Primus and Casillero del Diablo, among many more.

Huneeus began his career in his native country of Chile as CEO of Concha y Toro, but left the country due to political circumstances. Since then, he has been involved with large and small operations in the US, from heading all wine operations for Seagram, the one-time world leader of wines and spirits, to creating the Quintessa wine estate, to which he now dedicates his time. His family company, Huneeus Vintners, run by his son, Agustin Francisco, encompasses Quintessa, Faust and Illumination in Napa Valley; Flowers on the Sonoma Coast; and Veramonte, Neyen and Primus in Chile.

ABOUT CF NAPA BRAND DESIGN

For more than thirty-five years, CF Napa Brand Design has led the wine industry in innovation and originality. CF Napa's philosophy is based on one simple belief: Differentiated strategic positioning and evocative design combined with compelling storytelling are essential for establishing an emotional and cognitive connection between consumer and brand. The result has been brands with powerful positioning and compelling aesthetics, that consistently connect with consumers to increase market share, creating some of the most successful wine brands in the world.